OYSTER STEW

RICHARD E. SHEARER

PRESIDENT EMERITUS OF
ALDERSON-BROADDUS COLLEGE

LifeRich
PUBLISHING
an imprint of The Reader's Digest Association, Inc.

LifeRich Publishing books may be ordered
through booksellers or by contacting:

LifeRich Publishing
1663 Liberty Drive
Bloomington, IN 47403
www.liferichpublishing.com
1 (888) 238-8637

Because of the dynamic nature of the Internet, any web addresses or
links contained in this book may have changed since publication and
may no longer be valid. The views expressed in this work are solely those
of the author and do not necessarily reflect the views of the publisher,
and the publisher hereby disclaims any responsibility for them.

Any people depicted in stock imagery provided by Thinkstock are
models, and such images are being used for illustrative purposes only.
Certain stock imagery © Thinkstock.

ISBN: 978-1-4897-0101-5 (sc)
ISBN: 978-1-4897-0100-8 (hc)
ISBN: 978-1-4897-0099-5 (e)

Library of Congress Control Number: 2013922164

Printed in the United States of America.

LifeRich Publishing rev. date: 12/05/13

THE SHEARERS ARRIVING IN PHILIPPI 1950

DEDICATION

For all those who provided me with oyster stew or comparable encouragement, particularly my beloved wife, Ruth, and all other members of our family.

CONTENTS

Dedication...vii

Introduction...1

Oyster Stew 9

How My Family Handled Tragedy 13

A Disastrous Introduction 21

Ruth Mansberger Shearer 25

My First Christmas Present to My Bride 35

More about Rudy.. 41

Setting Sail... 49

Ruth Sparks Worldwide Travel and Lasting Friendships........ 61

An Angel on My Shoulder 71

Going My Way?... 81

Our Little Giant Has Fallen.................................. 85

The Next Generation... 89

Another First Lady and Scholar............................89

Our Other Little Giant 93

Our Best Mistake 97

Some Memorable Experiences and a Few Bits of Philosophy 103

My Only Deep Regret 103

A Visit to Haiti and to the Mellons...................... 105

Dealing with Racial Matters............................... 108

Broadening the Horizon 112

Why Did You Stay So Long? 116

A Year of Sad Travel... 120

True Religion 123

The Impact of Teachers 125

Memorial Day 2013 133

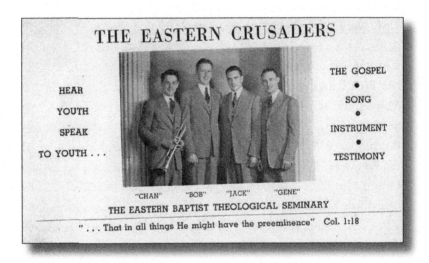

THE EASTERN CRUSADERS

HEAR
YOUTH
SPEAK
TO YOUTH . . .

THE GOSPEL
•
SONG
•
INSTRUMENT
•
TESTIMONY

"CHAN"   "BOB"   "JACK"   "GENE"
THE EASTERN BAPTIST THEOLOGICAL SEMINARY

" . . . That in all things He might have the preeminence"   Col. 1:18

THE EASTERN CRUSADERS
EASTERN BAPTIST SEMINARY (RICHARD SHEARER ON RIGHT)

INTRODUCTION

As I write these stories about my family, I have a slight feeling of guilt when I remember that my wife, Rudy, who was an excellent professor, often said to her classes as well as at home, "There is no good writing. There is only good *re-writing*." I have commented several times that I became president of Alderson-Broaddus College in December 1950 at the age of 30. However, sixty years have flown by, and I now write at the age of 93, which age makes me feel that I cannot re-write. I am glad for help through my good friend Barbara Smith, who taught writing at the college. Hopefully, she will correct some of my slips.

Most of these stories will focus on Ruth, but I will include some background on my own childhood and youth plus a few anecdotes about our children as they grew up on the college campus. There has been much more to our lives than the academic! I have chosen the title *Oyster Stew* because that gesture of my mother's represents the feeling of support I received from my parents, a feeling which has continued throughout my life. It includes the encouragement of my wife, Ruth, my family, and my teachers and colleagues in both church and education. Above all, because of the love of all of these people and because of their faith in me and in God, I have always felt a partnership with the Good Lord.

Throughout my thirty-three years in the college presidency, I received many personal letters from alumni, parents, and, of course, trustees and denominational leaders. One of my good friends and a true American Baptist leader, Luther Wesley Smith, wrote me every year to show his personal interest in what we were doing. In addition, one of my favorite professors was Norman Vincent Peale, who taught several courses in homiletics at New Brunswick Seminary. We developed a special friendship as I took him to the Pennsylvania Railroad station when classes ended and he needed to return to his pastorate of Marble Collegiate Church on Fifth Avenue in New York. I think the largest crowd to attend any convocation at Alderson-Broaddus gathered when Dr. Peale spoke at our Founders' Day celebration in 1982, shortly before I left the presidency. However, the most memorable letter I ever received over the many years at the college came from an alumna who graduated in the 1920s. Ellie Roberts married a classmate, Steve Roberts. Together they became an exceptionally effective educational team as they headed the Perkiomen School in Pennsylvania In 1970, Alderson-Broaddus received a grant from the Ford Foundation, and I persuaded Ellie and Steve to join us in getting ready for our centennial year in 1970. I also asked Steve to become our Director of Admissions. The Robertses were with us for almost four years. The memorable letter that she wrote to me came after Steve died and she was living in a nursing home in Hudson, Ohio, near their son. Her letter was typed, with many errors, but I shall never forget its message. "Dear Dick, I can't see, I can't hear, I can't walk, and I can't feel BUT I CAN REMEMBER

I want you to know that the happiest years of Steve's and my lives were when we were with you at A-B." That brief letter of appreciation will stay in my memory forever.

But let me summarize and introduce these stories by reprinting here an article written by our daughter, Suzanne Shearer Jones, and published in the Alderson-Broaddus College magazine in 1983. It reads as follows.

This Is Your Life: Dr. and Mrs. Shearer

Our story is one of a team, Dr. and Mrs. Shearer, a team of two people devoted to a lifetime ministry of Christian mission, of commitment, and of academic achievements.

In these days of so much transition and of so many people who don't seem to possess a loyalty to a cause—easily moving from one job to another for more money or more recognition—we stop to express our appreciation to a team who has not been "typical" of this present trend, but have maintained a cause—a Christian cause—for which they have been loyal for their lifetime.

We're sure it wasn't easy moving in that December 1950 blizzard to the small town of Philippi, leaving the "civilization" of New Brunswick, New Jersey, to come to "Virginia"—no, worse, West Virginia—relatively unknown in the East as a separate state and certainly not thought of as "almost heaven." Thirty years old—the youngest man ever to become a college president—bringing a wife and three babies under the age of five years to a new home.

But home is where the heart is and Alderson-Broaddus and West Virginia truly became home as year after year the Shearers worked hard as a team and believed in their cause—ignoring present-day trends by passing up many new and more financially attractive offers. Other academicians who knew of these offers to the Shearers never understood and would shake their heads in disbelief.

Let's look a little closer to gain some insight.

Dr. and Mrs. Shearer began as a team when they started dating in high school. Dr. Shearer was the son of a builder and devoted Connellsville Baptist Church family in Connellsville, Pennsylvania. Mrs. Shearer was the daughter of a Methodist minister and his wife, Arlie and Mame Mansberger.

Mrs. Shearer was the "city" girl and social butterfly in high school and Dr. Shearer was the "country" boy. Both extremely active—and competitive. Multi-talented from singing to wearing some of the first knickers at Connellsville High School, to rivaling Mrs. Shearer for class offices and high school valedictorian. (By the way, she edged him out for that spot.)

As most love affairs go, however, it got worse before it got better. But "our team" was meant to be, and whether it was the lamb cake that was left on the Mansbergers' porch one night to smooth over a disagreement or throwing stones at what was thought to be Mrs. Shearer's bedroom window one night only to discover Rev. Mansberger was the one awakened and not Rudy—(Good thing "Dear Old Dad" was a minister and dear son-in-law-to-be was in seminary at this time)—this frustrated love affair was to continue over a college and not between a man and woman.

So, our story continues from a beautiful hilltop in Philippi where Dr. and Mrs. Shearer made their home thirty-two years ago. We can look back and remember so many things:

a young and energetic college president learning to fly his own plane (an air coup) so that he could get more places faster—good and bad this aviation achievement has always allowed Dr. Shearer to double and triple schedule himself on behalf of the College. Many nights, family or staff would go to Philippi's grass field airport to shine their car lights on the field so that Dr. Shearer could land after dark.

a young and energetic woman who doubles and triples her schedule as mother of three, professor, hostess for the A-B campus, wife, and counselor for students. Her "West Virginia Mother of the Year Award" was well earned.

a dynamic and motivated college president who leads to build a campus from three buildings to fourteen, but more important, leads A-B to innovative programs year after year to make it the leader it is today in Christian higher education.

a dynamic teacher who commutes by bus to New York City and drags in late at night to her family living in a third floor attic apartment in New Jersey so that she can attain the highest degree in her teaching field—a doctorate in Education from Columbia University.

a proud college president who leads the College in receiving North Central Accreditation and drops a parachute with a baby doll attached (ribbon intact) saying "We made it" to share the news with the College family.

a proud educator as students taught by Mrs. Shearer take their places in the classroom as teachers themselves.

a human college president who enjoys the spirit of young people as they throw him in the College pond to celebrate a campus-wide achievement or as he fires a small cannon when the soccer team scores (one time hitting an A-B cheerleader—you gotta watch out for him) or treating the basketball team to steaks because of a significant victory.

a human wife and mother as family would tire of endless stops on vacations because of college business until one time, hot and tired she uttered: "Nobody's home—I hope, I hope," expressing how everyone in the car felt.

a talented college president and his wife who can sing, paint, decorate, play piano duets, create, teach, preach, write, be Mom and Dad, Grandma and Grandpa—and oh, yes—farm.

a caring college president and his wife who know the students on a first name basis, eat with students in the college cafeteria, share with students in their home—who triumph with students in their successes and grieve if there are tragedies or failures—but who care enough to take a stand when necessary, wanting students to grow and mature knowing that this is a part of their college experience. A president and his wife who care for faculty and parents and who care about the dual system of public and private education in America and that parents and students have a choice in matters of size of school and type of school.

and finally , *a spiritually committed college president and his wife* who study their religion, share their religion, and live their religion. For those who know Dr. and Mrs. Shearer personally, "turning the other cheek" has been one of their virtues. This "team" is committed to emphasizing a Christian lifestyle on the A-B campus—committed to American Baptists and to challenging them to support and believe in institutions of Christian higher education like A-B—as a mission—as one of the greatest sources of faith they can have in our young people who are our tomorrows!

It's not only a challenge—it's a ministry! And we thank Dr. and Mrs. Shearer for their life of service to others and for their steadfast devotion to this most important and honorable ministry—Christian higher education for our young people—faith in our tomorrows!

THE SHEARER FAMILY 1932
(L TO R: BROTHER HOWARD AND WIFE (JENNY), MOTHER
FLORENCE, GRANDMOTHER PRINKEY, RICHARD E. SHEARER,
GRANDMOTHER SHEARER, FATHER DENNIS, BROTHER PAUL)

OYSTER STEW

I GRADUATED FROM CONNELLSVILLE HIGH School in a class of 275. My girlfriend, Ruth Mansberger, daughter of the Methodist minister in our town, was the valedictorian, and I graduated sixth in the same senior class. My special interest throughout the four years of high school was forensics. I had won the extemporaneous speaking contest and was part of a successful debate team and had one of the leads in the Senior Class play, "Smilin' Through." Those were good years of education and preparation for later life,

I was still a country boy in home background, and the girl I was starting to fall in love with was more citified. But more about our courtship later.

My parents were insistent upon my going on to college, like my older brother, Howard, had done ten years ahead of me. He had graduated from California State Teachers College, majoring in Manual Training, and even though these were the '30s, the Depression years, he found work as a construction foreman. While he was still in college, he was the school photographer and was good-looking and popular.

As a young boy, my first ambition was to shovel ashes. As the youngest of five children, I stayed at home most of the time to do farm chores and to help my mother while my two older brothers, Howard and Paul, went with my father to help in his building projects and farm work.

Behind our house was an alley that led to our garage and barn, but it was unpaved. In rainy weather it would get very muddy, and my father and brothers would go to the nearby community of Coalbrook, where there was the longest line of coke ovens in the world. These ovens were the main source of coke for the steel mills in Pittsburgh. As a small boy I liked the fact that when my dad and brothers brought back a truckload of ashes, the road to our garage and barn looked a lot nicer and was easy to navigate. I wanted to do something in life that would improve the mud that existed not only in our road but perhaps in people's lives.

All through our family life, Bible reading and prayer were daily activities, each day closing with prayer on our knees. Sunday was full of church attendance, the First Baptist Church on Pittsburgh Street in Connellsville, both morning and evening and the little interdenominational church in our rural village of Poplar Grove in the afternoon. In addition to relatives coming regularly to visit us, we always welcomed ministers and teachers for Sunday dinner and other times. As I look back I can understand that many of these influences helped me feel a calling into the full-time Christian ministry. I'm sure my mother's prayers and guidance were also at the core of my decision. However, I was always thankful that neither of my parents influenced me unduly.

I won scholarships to both Bucknell College and Washington and Jefferson College, but the background of church involvement led me to decide to attend Eastern Baptist College and Seminary, located then in Rittenhouse Square in downtown Philadelphia, approximately three hundred miles from my home. The facility was modest but was home for several hundred of us who were dedicated to some phase of Christian ministry. We were like family, all of us working hard to earn much of our way through college and seminary and also to prepare well for our vocation.

Bob Acker and Pete Hill and I lived in the fifth-floor "penthouse." There were no elevators, so as we ran up and down the stairs several times each day, we got ample exercise. The downtown location also provided many wonderful opportunities for practical work assignments. Mine included going every Thursday night by subway and then across the bridge to Camden, where Bob and I worked under the guidance of Miss Hatch, the missionary in charge. For two years, our job was to round up a number of young people who were walking the streets, invite them to come in to play basketball and then to join in prayer and Bible study. Many of my other assignments involved music, including directing the choir at the Greenhill Presbyterian Church in Wilmington, Delaware. A member of the DuPont family attended there, but that is a whole story of its own.

Of course, in those Depression days, students did not own cars. Fortunately; hitchhiking was expected of many college students. When Christmas vacation came, I joined a number of other students in working at Railway Express in downtown Philadelphia. We earned good money for a brief time, and the Express folk, handling most of the Christmas packages being sent both near and far, appreciated us. When we finished work with them, we headed home for a brief vacation. For me, for several years, that meant hitchhiking nearly three hundred miles. The Pennsylvania Turnpike had not been built yet, and getting through the line of suburbs on Route 30 was the hardest part of the trip. Of course, getting over the mountains wasn't easy either, particularly on cold winter nights. And then there was the problem of getting off Route 30 to get to Connellsville. Fortunately, drivers back then knew that most hitchhikers were students and other honest folk. I met many fine people by using my thumb, and I always tried to show appreciation.

I remember, however, that quite a number of times I would not get home until around 3:00 a.m., and at least at Christmastime, it was usually a cold, snowy morning. What a joy to be home, and what a welcome from my mother, who was always up waiting for me, regardless of the time. And, yes, she had my favorite soup, oyster stew, ready and waiting. That was a gesture of love that is written indelibly in my life story.

THE FIRST BAPTIST CHURCH OF CONNELLSVILLE, PENNSYLVANIA

HOW MY FAMILY
HANDLED TRAGEDY

THERE WERE FIVE CHILDREN IN the Shearer family, and I was the youngest. Only three of us survived. Karl died of diphtheria before I was born. Ila Merlene died of meningitis. One Sunday she was in church with the rest of us, and the next Sunday she was gone. She had taken care of me as a baby, and I felt her loss deeply.

My brother Paul, who was five years older than I, had a nervous breakdown, serious enough that my parents took him to a psychiatrist and then to the mental hospital in Torrence. He was given various medications and electric shock treatment, but these did not help much.

I was with Paul during his breakdown. The family had been visiting relatives, and two of my cousins and I decided to go to the Livingston store in Mill Run, the only location for socializing on a Saturday night. We had been there for a while before I said to Paul, "Eugene and I are going to visit Aunt and Uncle Shipley, and you can come with us."

Paul shook his head. "I'll come later," he said.

Half an hour later, he came running down the road, hysterical with fear, just literally out of his mind. It was all Eugene and I could do to hold him, he was so scared. We never knew what caused this panic. After treatment he did settle down to the point that he could be at home, but there were times when he suffered greatly, and so did the whole family.

After my parents died, Paul became sort of a ward of the state. Instead of putting such individuals into institutions, the state contracted with families to take these people into their homes. Various members of the family visited often and took him for outings, and he did well under most circumstances. However, he could not be left alone, could not be trusted always to behave appropriately. My mother, until she died at age 71, gave much of her life to him, for she and my dad would not allow for him to be institutionalized.

My oldest brother, Howard, was called H.D. when we were young. At California State Teachers College there in Pennsylvania, he developed an excellent reputation in acting and other arts. The drama coach even offered to take him to Hollywood, but he wanted to be a builder. He married a girl from LaTrobe, but it wasn't a good marriage. They had a daughter, a true sweetheart, and then lost a couple of children. Another daughter survived, but she became a problem, feeling that she wasn't truly wanted and therefore was unhappy and made others unhappy.

My parents, in dealing with Howard's wife and anyone else who hurt others, always just turned their backs and pretended innocence on the part of the perpetrator. They just trusted other people and the Lord.

Mountain folk up near Mill Run were all farmers. My mother was born into the Prinkey family, one of five girls and three boys. My dad was born into the Shearer family which included five boys and two girls. Grandfather Prinkey owned two beautiful farms up in the mountains. He also owned the only grist mill in Mill Run. The family was more well-to-do than many of their neighbors. The Shearers were just the opposite, having to work very hard just to make a living on their rocky farm. Mother went to Normal School and taught in a one-room school in Normalville before she married my father.

One catastrophe struck the Prinkey family, a tragedy which affected several generations.

I never knew either of my grandfathers, both of whom died before I was born. In the case of Grandfather Prinkey, he and a neighbor disagreed about a property line, and the neighbor hit Grandfather in the head with a fence rail. Grandfather was found unconscious. He recovered briefly but was never the same. When he failed to appear one day for dinner, he was found again unconscious, this time at the mill. The Prinkeys never revealed who it was who had struck Grandfather. They never sought revenge. They simply went to the Lord and the church for comfort.

My father was a very creative, forward-looking father and husband. My mother and dad were the first of the family to move down from the mountains to the little rural community of Poplar Grove, a country-town suburb of Connellsville.

My two brothers, when they were able, worked with my dad, helping to build houses and do farm work. He worked in the Trotter mine until he went out on his own, basically to become a fine decorative painter. He painted our sanctuary in the First Baptist Church as well as those of other churches, many of them very high and dangerous in terms of access. Until the last couple of decades, the organ pipes still held evidence of his talent and determination. People liked him, and he liked people.

Dad also worked for a funeral home, but he was allergic to the embalming fluid and therefore developed asthma. During the Depression, he did anything possible to keep the family together and healthy. We had cows and chickens and hogs, the latter being butchered the day after Thanksgiving.

We had a fruit cellar with concrete walls. We didn't have freezers in those days, so the fruit cellar had to serve our needs. My mother canned a lot of vegetables and fruit and even meat. We were self-supportive except for sugar and flour.

In terms of appearance, my parents were good-looking, a

very handsome couple. My father was well built and always well groomed. Mother was a woman of average size with curly gray hair. She always wore dresses, some called "house dresses." Better clothes were saved for church and special occasions.

As I look back over my childhood, I sense that I was closest to my mother, and H.D. and Paul were my father's helpers until, of course, Paul had his breakdown. At the time, having graduated from high school, Paul was working for the Firestone Company in Connellsville—his first and only job. Howard, on the other hand, worked with Dad at intervals, but after college, he secured a foreman's job with the Ragnor-Benson Company in Pittsburgh and was given an early assignment helping to build the Tuscarora Tunnel on the Pennsylvania Turnpike.

When that job was finished, Howard was responsible for building the Healthorama at a hospital in Pittsburgh. Long-range, he was in charge of building high-rise parking garages in downtown locations from Bangor, Maine, all over the east.

The neighbors always knew us, too, as musicians. My father and brothers were all musical. As the youngest of the three boys, and as soon as I was able to stand up on the piano bench, they included me in the family quartet, and we practiced regularly to sing at church services and at funerals. I sang the melody, my father sang the tenor part, Howard was the baritone, and Paul sang bass. Music was almost as central in our family as farming, but of course farming took precedence over all avocations.

Another primary interest was camping. This was the way we spent our summer vacations. My parents spent one entire winter making a large tent, which must have been at least 12' x 24' inside. I remember my mother sewing dozens of eyelets for fasteners to hold up the skirt that went around all four sides of the tent. It was built so that, when we didn't need privacy, we could remove the skirt and have cool air throughout the tent, which was divided into two rooms so that another family could sleep in half the tent while we used the other. Usually we took a family with us into Newell's Grove just below the Indian Creek Baptist Church. Quite often numerous relatives came to enjoy the evening dinner and campfire, which brought us all together to toast marshmallows and tell stories. On several occasions we had forty or more people for supper, and although the visitors brought covered dishes, my mother and father were the chief providers and did most of the work. There was a long table that my father constructed, which he also used regularly in his wallpapering assignments. I often felt that my parents would need to return home to recuperate.

THE SHEARER FAMILY, FRIENDS, AND HOMEMADE TENT

A number of years later my father bought a piece of ground in a wooded area at White, Pennsylvania, close to Mill Run and Normalville. He and my brothers built a cabin and a beautiful outdoor fireplace in the woods. From then on, giving up on the tent, our vacations were a little easier for them to handle.

When we were traveling, Rudy and our children loved to get

off the Donegal exit of the Pennsylvania Turnpike to head to that inimitable camp site.

In the meantime, as I grew up, my mother was my guide, and I was given responsibilities both in the kitchen and on the farm, always encouraged in my education. My first job on the farm was delivering milk to the neighborhood. In a sense, we were the local dairy for the community of Poplar Grove. I later learned to milk the cows myself, always by hand. As I grew older, my brothers and I hoed corn on a rocky hillside on the forty-acre farm that my father rented. I remember H.D. saying one day, as we hoed on the hillside that had a view toward Dawson, Pennsylvania, that when Sarah B. Cochran lit a light in her tower in Dawson, you could read a newspaper from our hilltop. I know he was exaggerating, but I learned later that Sarah Cochran became a major donor for Bethany College in West Virginia. I believe she made her money through the coal business.

As for tragedy, two others occurred even before the breakdown of Paul. My two siblings died well before that. My parents were never bitter about those losses but instead turned their grief to helpfulness. Our home was almost a community center on Saturday nights, when neighbors would come to share their problems and also to listen to our famous cuckoo clock chime every hour and every half hour. My parents were helpers wherever help was needed.

THE MANSBERGER FAMILY
(FRONT ROW, GRANDCHILDREN; SECOND ROW L TO R: SISTER
BETTY, RUTH, FATHER ARLIE, MOTHER MAME, BROTHER
ARLIE'S WIFE (ELLEN), SISTER VIVIAN; BACK ROW L TO R:
BROTHER ARLIE, SISTER VIVIAN'S HUSBAND (FLOYD))

A Disastrous
Introduction

I WAS STILL A STUDENT in Philadelphia at Eastern Baptist College and Seminary. Their academic program at that time consisted of four years of college, granting the Bachelor of Arts degree, and then two of seminary, granting the Bachelor of Theology degree—a total of six years at the same institution.

As mentioned earlier, in the collegiate years I did a lot of hitchhiking. Fortunately, as the Depression lessened, I was able to secure a 1936 Plymouth sedan to get me places both around Philadelphia as well as home to Connellsville.

My opportunities to see my fiancee, Ruth Mansberger, were very infrequent, and when her father began the pastorate of the First Methodist Church of Weirton, West Virginia, that even lengthened the distance between us. However, it did not lessen our amorous interest in each other.

I think it was during my last year at Eastern Seminary and over the Christmas break that I determined to make my first trip to Weirton to visit the Mansberger family, especially to see Ruth. She was already teaching in Weirton High School, commuting to Pittsburgh, beginning her master's degree work at the University of Pittsburgh. That first visit to Weirton and to the Mansberger manse proved to be disastrous in a number of ways, but not detrimental to our continuing courtship.

The long drive from Philadelphia found me wrestling with automobile problems as I approached Weirton. Every time I went down a hill and put the brakes on, my headlights went out, which was dangerous and delayed my travel, for I was afraid to go at regular speed. I finally arrived in Weirton at around two o'clock in the morning, not knowing where the Methodist parsonage was located. I found the police station and asked for help. A cordial officer took me to the church, which had a small house behind it.

I wondered how I could get entrance without waking the entire family. The house was mainly a bungalow with an additional half-story, and I surveyed the situation from all sides. Finally I found an open window, and when I got close, I couldn't hear any snoring, which made me think I had found Ruth's bedroom.

I found a tall garbage can and dragged it to the window, then climbed onto it. I couldn't see into the room but still hoped it might just be Ruth's. I called gently, "Rudy, Rudy, it's Dick," but no one answered. Rather impetuously, I started climbing in, still not wanting to waken the whole family. However good my intentions, they did not work out.

A light went on, and Reverend Mansberger yelled for help louder than he had ever preached from the pulpit. In fact, he was scared to death. Lights went on all over the house, and it took considerable time for them to realize who it was and to give me acceptance. Rudy interceded for me as much as she could, but it was hard for her to interpret this dramatic entrance of her suitor. They gave me a blanket and allowed me to spend the rest of the night on the sofa in the living room. I slept little that night, and I think the Mansbergers also went sleepless.

The next morning things had calmed down a little, but there wasn't much cordial conversation at the breakfast table. Reverend Mansberger mentioned that there had been an article in the paper a day or two earlier warning the people of Weirton about night prowlers and notifying citizens to be on the lookout. Of course this made my entry doubly unwelcome and upsetting.

As we finished breakfast, I put a dollar under my plate, and Ruth and I spent a little time together, but I didn't stay very long. I think I can understand, as I look back now, why Mother Mansberger questioned the judgment of her daughter. She wasn't at all happy about having been tipped for her services.

A year or so went by, and then we planned our wedding in the church in Weirton, but it took many more years for Ruth's mother to accept me fully. Her parents had looked on the exterior of the situation, but Ruth considered the intention and gave me credit at least for that.

I think also that the family tide started turning solidly in my direction when I stood with Ruth's father, the Reverend Doctor Mansberger, and my uncle, The Reverend Lindley Shearer, in front of the sanctuary of the First Methodist Church in Weirton and sang the lovely wedding number "Because," with my bride standing in the back of the sanctuary, waiting to come down the aisle to be married. This was Ruth's idea, and I believe it helped to demonstrate that this young minister she was about to marry had both talent and determination.

RICHARD E. AND RUTH M. SHEARER WEDDING, JUNE 16, 1944

Ruth Mansberger Shearer

RUDY WAS NICKNAMED WHILE IN college. We first met in an Ancient History class taught by Miss Walker in Connellsville High School when we were freshmen in 1933. Those were years when our country was in a deep economic depression, but her father was minister of the Central Methodist Church in Connellsville, and my dad and mother managed a small farm. My dad at first also worked in the Trotter coal mines, finally getting into the field in which he was most talented, construction.

The love notes that Ruth and I sent back and forth in Miss Walker's class became a prelude to a much more serious courtship, a love affair of a country boy and a city girl, with her parents very skeptic of the boy. In turn, my parents were hopeful that the relationship in bloom would blossom fully. My gifts to Ruth on several occasions of Dentyne chewing gum were to her parents not impressive.

My mother was helpful in the transition. She had a mold in which she could pour cake batter and end up with a beautiful cake in the shape of a lamb. She would cover it with coconut, put eyes of raisins in it, and it would become the talk of the village. One day I asked if she would make one of those cakes and let me give it to Ruth and her family. She happily obliged. When I took it to the Methodist parsonage, I stealthily approached the back porch, rang the bell, and left the cake at the door and ran. I'm not sure why I ran except I just wanted her to have the cake. She later expressed appreciation both to me and my mother and said that her family laughed about the gift and still called her "Lambie." Nevertheless, the cake was appreciated by the Mansbergers and maybe helped them to see my affection on a higher plane.

One day long after we were married, she mentioned in a college class that we dated for seven years before we were married. She told me that she thought the students would appreciate knowing that and would respect it, but she said that as a total class, they laughed. We knew then that the idea of a lengthy courtship was not in the minds of those students.

Even though Ruth and I were happy in the pastorate at the First Baptist Church of New Brunswick, New Jersey, we decided for our long-range career destiny to prepare for college administration positions and a professorship. Ruth said to me one day, "Dick, if faculty members at a college are to respect us, in whatever positions we obtain, we can't cut our preparation short. We must be willing to show them we have the discipline and ability to prepare well through graduate work. Otherwise we will not have the respect of those who work with us." I agreed and spent the following five years, while we were in the New Brunswick pastorate, commuting to New York to earn graduate degrees at Teachers College at Columbia. At the same time, all three of our children were born there in New Brunswick, two years apart. Later, as they got older, Ruth finished her doctorate also at Teachers College and graduated with distinction.

Two personal instances happened while we were graduate students. The first is in regard to several of my professorial contacts. Ruth and I both liked our professors at TC and drank in all the lessons we could learn from them. Our professors learned that we were in the ministry. Two of them opened up at different times to me about their religious background. Dr. Henry Lynn, who taught several courses in school planning said to me after class one day, "You know, Dick, I wish I had the faith of my mother." I said I was glad he felt that way and hoped he would give Christian faith a real try.

In somewhat like manner, Dr. Karl Bigelow, my major professor, who helped establish school systems in parts of Africa and was an authority in his field, but also a perfectionist in many ways, said to me one day after class, "I don't go to church anymore, Dick. My parents made me go to Sunday school and church, and I resented it. That has affected my concept of church ever since."

Again I responded not critically but said, "Dr. Bigelow, I hope as an adult now, you will take another look at faith and church-going."

Ruth had some interesting experiences with professors also but on a somewhat different subject. As a doctoral candidate, she was in a seminar led by Dr. Max Wise, who was very demanding of his students. When Rudy returned home each day, she would tell me what had happened in Dr. Wise's class, and several events were particularly memorable to both of us. She said that as they started the seminar composed of all doctoral students, Dr. Wise asked them to say where they were from and where they hoped to serve eventually. Ruth mentioned that she was from Alderson-Broaddus College in Philippi, West Virginia. Dr. Wise wasn't afraid to embarrass his students and said to the class, "Has anyone ever heard of Alderson-Broaddus College or Philippi, West Virginia?"

Ruth said she held her head low, thinking his question unfair. However, one young man in the class raised his hand and said, "Dr. Wise, I know about both. I've been there." In at least some way, Dr. Wise himself felt "put in his place." Ruth said afterwards that she felt like hugging the young man who had made the comment and whom she didn't know. She found later that he was a Baptist with some responsibility in missions. She thanked him profusely.

Another incident in the same seminar involved Ruth at the center. As the class proceeded, one of the assignments was for each student to write a paper on a chosen subject and to read it to the class. Dr. Wise always had one penetrating question. When Ruth read her report, he asked it of her also: "What's your proof of that statement?"

Ruth said that after each session of the seminar, the class would go to a snack bar for something to drink and to talk and laugh over the class. Deep down, however, they were frightened by and of Dr. Wise. When he asked Ruth his favorite question, she answered almost automatically, "A typical Wise question." The class burst into laughter, and so did Dr. Wise. Ruth said that little incident changed the entire mood of the seminar and made it a much happier experience than it could have been. Some years later, when Dr. Wise left Teachers College and became head of the Danforth Foundation in St. Louis, he wrote to Ruth and me, suggesting that if there was an area in which his foundation could help us as we expanded academic programs, he would help us write an application to his foundation. As a result, Alderson-Broaddus received a grant of $230,000 to be used in the advancement of the institution. I was happy to report that not only did we receive that fine grant but that MY RUTH WAS RESPONSIBLE FOR IT. I always felt that if I had not been married to Ruth, and if our destiny had not already been set at A-B, she might have been chosen as one of the Teachers College professors.

An honor she did receive in 1974 was being chosen as West Virginia Mother of the Year. I'm not sure of the criteria used for the selection, but it was very appropriate both in our area as well as for Ruth. Anna Jarvis was the person who founded Mother's Day in Webster, about six miles from where we lived. West Virginia is especially proud of the Mother's Day events that now take place even internationally. I can guess some of the reasoning of the statewide committee designated to make the selection, but

I have never seen a formal listing such as "competent, loving, and capable mother."

Ruth was asked to speak at the Mother's Day church in Grafton on that Mother's Day in 1974. She was nervous about it, as she was about all her speaking assignments. She said, "I feel relaxed in a classroom, but I am on edge when I stand to make a speech." She said that one of the reasons she felt uneasy about speechmaking was that she worried about what she left out and should have included. I told her I felt just the opposite. I didn't feel completely at home in the classroom but did feel somewhat accomplished at the podium. I think to a great degree the feelings on both of our parts were those we had become accustomed to.

I said, "Honey, you do a good job, and you're better than you think you are." And she was. The congregation gave her a standing ovation when she finished and were very appreciative of her thoughtful comments on motherhood.

I think any measure of our children's development would support the characteristic of Ruth's competent and loving motherhood. Our daughter Pat has a doctor's degree in education, has been a school principal in Urbana, Illinois, and is now First Lady with her presidential husband, Dick Wilson, at Illinois Wesleyan University. Our second daughter, Suzanne, has been married to a dentist, Dr. Terry Jones, who served in VA hospitals both in Germany and in Huntington, West Virginia, and herself has been an honored case worker at Health South Hospital in Huntington for over twenty years. Our third child, Richard Judson, has been involved in many parts of the world in the chemical industry and is now the CEO of Emerge Energy Service, headquartered in Fort Worth.

One event that demonstrates Ruth's strong character occurred during a celebration in the local community. Each fall at Homecoming for the college, we had a parade downtown. We took this very seriously and enjoyed exciting the local community about the college and welcoming back alumni. We could always trust Blaine Corder to provide us with the music and pageantry of the Philippi Middle School band. Many civic leaders marched with the college leadership, some riding in convertible cars. Ruth and I were perched in the back seat of one of those in 1974, the same year that Ruth was designated West Virginia Mother of the Year. While we rode slowly by, a lady ran up to the car, shaking her finger at Ruth and saying, "You're not worthy of being Mother of the Year. I have more children than you have."

As we rode by, Ruth smiled and quickly, simply, answered, "Good for you."

Another much earlier experience, a trek across the United States, provided a great illustration of Rudy's character.

The first special trip, before any of our children were born, took us across the country in a make-shift trailer that my brother had put together from the bed of a truck. It certainly wasn't fancy, but it had running water and two bedsprings on the sides that opened up when we wanted to sleep. During the day the structure looked more like a horse trailer than one for people, so we had to respond to people asking to see our animals. At night the contraption looked like a tent on wheels. We agreed that we would use this apparition six nights a week but rent a motel room on the seventh so that we could get showers and rest. We also agreed that we would eat breakfast and lunch in the trailer but dinner at a restaurant. Quite often we would say, "When we see the next tree, we'll stop in the shade and eat." That proved to be almost impossible because there were miles and miles between trees.

We stopped in Scottsdale, Arizona, to see our seminary friends, Andy and Jean Anderson, who were pastoring the Baptist church there. He was a good singer, a tenor, and had joined me in traveling from the seminary in Philadelphia to Wilmington, Delaware, over the two-year period while I was choir director at the Green Hill Presbyterian Church. Jean was also a graduate of the seminary and was a wonderful minister's wife. That visit was a great break in our journey.

We then headed across the desert for California. My Chevrolet wasn't used to that degree of heat, however, and boiled over several times. Nevertheless, we made the trip without serious incident.

We also had friends to visit in La Havre on the outskirts of Los Angeles—Bill and Mae Powell. They were probably my closest friends in seminary, and when Rudy came from Western Maryland College to see me, they made her feel at home in their house in Conshohocken. On the cross-country trip we also visited Terry and Gloria Croskrey, who had been deeply involved in our first pastorate at Atlantic Highlands, New Jersey. Terry was in the service, helping to man the radar on Sandy Hook during World War II. They became close friends, and I recently sent Gloria a card honoring her 89th birthday.

We decided to return via a northern route, going to Reno and then to the Dakotas, where we wanted to see Mt. Rushmore. The climb to that spot in the mountains overheated the car, and we had to make several stops before reaching our destination.

We returned to New Brunswick within the month allotted for our vacation and resumed church and community duties to the full, glad that we had seen our country from east to west and back again. Throughout almost the entire adventure—except for a few moments of frustration or fatigue—Rudy was eager, curious, hard-working, and good-natured—typical of her lifelong attitude.

A second special trek the next year proved less fulfilling and illustrates Rudy's concern for her parents as well as our difficulty in having me accepted as a worthy son-in-law. Rudy was pregnant with our first child, but she was determined to make the trip to Canada. We thought it would be good to take her parents, who had always wanted to travel.

We didn't have our homemade trailer any longer, so I arranged to make the front seats in our Pontiac turn all the way down, so that if we got caught in the country without motels, Rudy and I could rest for the night in the car.

I'm not sure of our exact location, probably somewhere between Toronto and Montreal. We had already enjoyed Niagara Falls and found ourselves on a country road at night, with a few farmsteads indicating rooms for rent. I followed one of the lanes and ended up in a barnyard near a house. We knocked on the door, and a friendly farm couple greeted us, indicating that they had only one room available. I said to Ruth, "I think we'd better take it for your parents. You and I can sleep in the car." She agreed.

After some sleep and a good breakfast with the farm couple, we headed into a more populated area. The Rev. Dr. Mansberger, Rudy's dad, quietly accepted the whole experience, but his wife, Mame, felt otherwise. She was upset all day about the fact that I had parked in the barnyard and forced my pregnant wife to walk through questionable soil and then sleep in the car. Ruth accepted the conditions more kindly and tried to persuade her mother that all was well.

On the second night, as we drove through a small Canadian city, I inquired about accommodations and was given directions to the most expensive hotel in town. I drove up, parked, and went in to register all four of us. When I came out to tell the family that we were all set, Mame asked how much it was going to cost. I told her we would pay for it, but when she insisted upon knowing the amount and heard it, she said she wouldn't sleep all night at that cost. She meant it, and I knew it, so we drove on to a small motel and enjoyed a good night's sleep.

It rained that night, and water came down into the closet where Mame had hung her clothes. This added considerably to her negativity.

I am not sure of all the scenes we saw in Canada because the tone of the trip had been set and remained with us even after we got home. Fortunately, Rudy stayed well, and both her father and her mother, over time, became more appreciative of me as well as the trip.

Again, Ruth was always a good mediator, always concerned for others—and for me.

Merry Christmas

The Shearers

NEWLYWEDS' CHRISTMAS CARD 1944

MY FIRST CHRISTMAS
PRESENT TO MY BRIDE

RUTH AND I WERE MARRIED on June 16, 1944. I had already accepted the pastorate of Central Baptist Church in Atlantic Highlands, New Jersey, actually having begun there while I was finishing my senior year at Eastern Baptist Seminary. For the spring term, I commuted on week ends from Philadelphia to lead in their Sunday services.

After our honeymoon at Lake George, New York, Ruth joined me in Atlantic Highlands, where we began residence in the parsonage on Highland Avenue, right next to the church itself.

I knew this wasn't an easy move for Ruth, particularly because I had been in the church for a few months as a single minister. Our activities at the church had flourished, including a Thursday night "canteen" for servicemen who were serving in different nearby locations. One of the couples who came faithfully were Terry and Gloria Croskrey, who were from California. Terry was assigned as a member of the guard of the New York harbor, with the unit established on Sandy Hook, overlooking the harbor from the New Jersey side. In addition, our Wednesday night mid-week Bible study group had doubled in size quickly, with quite a number of young women participating, interested, perhaps, in knowing the single pastor. When Ruth settled with me in the

35

parsonage, our mid-week group attendance dropped to half of its previous number.

In the wintertime, the city of Atlantic Highlands blocked off Highland Avenue, which ran past the parsonage and the church. The young people of the town were able to use that venue for sled-riding. Because both of us were in our early twenties, we were happy to join the sled-riders on cold and snowy nights, sometimes ending up in the parsonage for hot chocolate.

Ruth and I had a real love for each other, proven by a courtship of more than seven years through both high school and college, but we also had differences in background and personal interests. I had been raised with a conservative and practical bent, whereas she (partly because of her small size of only five feet) was determined to excel, as evidenced by her academic achievement—valedictorian in our high school class and also winning the Outstanding Female Student Award at Western Maryland College.

As we moved close to our first Christmas together, I wondered what I should buy my bride. What I selected will reveal this practical tendency on my part versus the more personal gift that my wife would have chosen. I sought something that would make her comfortable when we went sled-riding, so I went to the city of Red Bank, where there were numerous gift shops. I ended up in Kislin's Army and Navy Store, purchasing what I thought would be a unique gift—a pair of ski pants that were just her size. I was excited about the gift, which would be my first Christmas present after marriage.

Christmas morning arrived, and I don't remember what she gave me, but I do remember her reaction to my "thoughtful" offering. She tried to cover her feelings by thanking me and saying how my gift would be useful, at least on sled-riding occasions. However, I could tell there was disappointment. Several years later she confessed to this and said that she had hoped for something like a piece of jewelry. Later I bought her a Bulova wristwatch and a full-carat diamond ring to replace the one which I had bought with the small amount of money I had saved from selling my trombone.

I am happy that over the forty-eight years of our married life, the differences in background and strength welded rather than separating us. When I performed weddings for other couples, I used our illustration to say that if you learn to understand and appreciate each other's differences, you will be a strong couple. However, it is important to have common ambitions and likenesses, similarities that brought you together in the first place.

My Ruth definitely built on what we had in common, particularly our goals. Even though her first visit to West Virginia and to Philippi left Ruth tentative, she soon gave herself heart and soul to three main purposes. The first was her husband. I always felt her strong support in many of my undertakings, even some somewhat risky. That support included preparing thoroughly for our educational leadership, full commitment to being a good mother of our three wonderful children, and a committed but balanced life as a college professor. I have not studied the educational landscape thoroughly enough to be sure of this fact, but she may have been the first college president's wife to become engaged fully in an important role at the college.

One phrase that Ruth repeated often and that I liked was emphasized by her when we chose to build our own home on the farm which we had purchased from Lester Holbert. The house was built on a knoll overlooking much of the college campus, even though it is a little distance from it. Quite often in the morning, particularly when Ruth would go to play our baby-grand piano, she would look out the bay window and comment, both to the family and to visitors, "This is our life." That phrase never left her. It showed deep personal commitment far beyond the skepticism with which she began our years in the mountains.

Another phrase that I always liked to hear Ruth utter represented our early love for each other and the maturing of that love into marriage, family, and careers. That phrase was, "I knew better than my parents." I considered that comment a compliment to me, and I know she meant it that way. As I've said elsewhere in my writings, her parents, particularly her mother, had questions about Dick Shearer. Her mother said, "If you marry that young minister you'll just end up in Flatwoods." That was a little country town not far from Connellsville where I supplied a pulpit for one summer. I think I won the full approval of both her mother and father by the time we moved to the First Baptist Church in New Brunswick and later into the college, but that took a number of years. I thought of my father, who had to win his way in order to secure the hand in marriage of my mother, who was part of one of the more affluent farm families in Mill Run, Pennsylvania. Again, that phrase, "I knew better than my parents," is indelibly written in my mind and heart, and I thank Ruth for repeating it often over the years.

RICHARD SHEARER PREACHING EASTER SERMON
FIRST BAPTIST CHURCH, NEW BRUNSWICK, NEW JERSEY
(RUTH BORN ON EASTER SUNDAY, MIDDLE-NAMED "EASTER")

MORE ABOUT RUDY

RUTH MANSBERGER AND I WERE married for forty-eight years. She was a supportive, inspirational, capable, and loving partner—and much, much more.

Before we were married, she had already distinguished herself academically. I remember on several occasions she made the comment, "I believe I am an attractive young lady, but I know I'll never win any beauty contests, and neither will I achieve renown as an athlete. I can, though, excel academically, and I will." And so she did, becoming a favorite student to all of her teachers and professors.

At the same time, she was very popular with the male population in both high school and college. Even as a Methodist minister's daughter, and although a number of limits were placed on social activities of young people, she became a good dancer and stepped over the traces by going to the movies.

As a member of the Girl Reserves, a helpful group in high school, she was asked, along with other members of her group, to usher at one movie, perhaps the first one she ever attended. When it was all over, she said, "I enjoyed that. I couldn't see anything wrong with it." While her parents were afraid this would be highly criticized in the church, they did not prohibit her from attending other select films.

She chose to attend Western Maryland College in Westminster, Maryland, because it had a good academic and liberal arts reputation and had been founded by the Methodist Protestant denomination, of which her father was a member and minister.

At the same time, I was attending Eastern Baptist College and Seminary. There were many talented girls there, particularly in the fields of music and Christian Education. In those years very few females thought of entering the pastoral ministry. Many of these young ladies ended up being wives of pastors and leaders in their churches. I dated several of them, but not seriously. Ruth Mansberger was still the apple of my eye. Even before I had a car I hitchhiked south and west through Riesterstown, Maryland, and on to Westminster to see her. Several times I was left by my kind drivers at the east side of Main Street in Westminster, which meant I had a mile to walk with my bag because the college was at the other end of town. Needless to say, I learned to pack lightly.

Ruth had many close college friends around her, for she had social magnetism. However, she was always glad to see me and to host me for part of the week end. She graduated summa cum laude and also won the Mary Ward Lewis Prize, which was given to the most outstanding female graduate.

After her graduation, Ruth joined her parents in Weirton, West Virginia, started teaching high school there, and began commuting to take her master's work at the University of Pittsburgh. I had two more years to finish the seminary program at Eastern. For most of these two years our relationship was interrupted with other interests. I spent my summers in several interesting ways: one summer I was weigh-master at the stockyard in Uniontown, Pennsylvania. I noticed how the farmers would get their cattle to drink as much water as possible before they got on the scales. That was o.k. with me, as weigh-master, but when they talked with me about tipping the scales in their favor, I drew a line and said, "You'll get exactly what they weigh and no more." I think the owners of the stockyard were grateful for my honesty.

I also spent a summer as a counselor at the Herman Cohn YMCA camp in Winston-Salem, North Carolina. Herman Cohn was a wealthy textile manufacturer in that area, where the textile industry flourished. This camp was well attended, mostly by high-school-aged young people. Since they needed extra life guards for the swimming area, they invited some of us to come a week early to take a Senior Life Guard course, thus to be able to supervise the waterfront. It wasn't an easy course, but I wanted the life guard certification and finished it.

A third summer I spent at home with a little Ford coupe that my father bought me. I sold Old Honesty soap, which was manufactured in Pittsburgh. I remember getting little boxes of samples. It was unique in those days in that there was bluing in the soap chips. I asked my mother to try it in her Maytag washer. When the laundry was finished, she looked at it and said, "I think it's a good product, Son." I took that recommendation to a number of households where I sold a considerable amount of the product. As I remember, at the same time that summer, I also filled the pulpit at the little Flatwoods Baptist Church about ten miles from my home in Connellsville.

It is true that during those summers, we saw little of each other, and I knew Ruth was rather seriously dating Don Espy, who was working for an oil company and already had a good income. After a trip down the Shenandoah Valley, they even got engaged. I soon learned my lesson and got back to building our relationship so that Ruth broke the engagement. As she said later, "We met in an Ancient History class as freshmen in high school, and we've been making history every since."

One very personal incident I have hesitated to share, but I believe Ruth would not mind. One night soon after we were married and moved into the parsonage in Atlantic Highlands, New Jersey, Ruth couldn't sleep. Finally she got up, dressed, and said, "Dick, I'm leaving you. I can't be happy here."

I quickly answered, "Honey, it's too early for us to make a harsh decision like that. We need more time together and also with the church people. However, whatever you do, I'll still be here for you." I felt I had to let her do whatever was on her mind.

She told me later what she did. "I went down to the railroad station and sat there alone. trying to think things through." She said no one was in the station at that early morning hour. However, a cat came and rubbed against her legs, purring in a friendly way. She said further, "That cat will never know what he meant to me that night. I sat for several hours and decided to come back to the parsonage. However, you handled me just right, letting me make my own decision, and I decided to give our marriage as well as the work in the church more time." I tried to understand her uncertainties and determined to strengthen our bond. Fortunately, she did likewise.

Approximately a year later, we were invited by the pulpit committee of the First Baptist Church of New Brunswick to visit them and to discuss the possibility of becoming their new minister, following Dr. Gilman, who had led the church through the sale of a downtown site and building a beautiful new church on Livingston Avenue, a main thoroughfare leading out of the city to the north and located near the city high school and also the Jewish synagogue. The Executive Minister of the New Jersey Baptist Convention, Dr. Roy Deere, had consulted with us earlier about his recommendation to the pulpit committee. He said, "I had a list of prospects to review with them, but I always ended up with you folk at the top of the list, even though I knew you were very young for this pastorate." We were both just twenty-four years old. Our discussion with the pulpit committee went favorably, and they indicated that they were ready to recommend us at a church business meeting.

After they reported their intentions, I said, "Would you please give Ruth and me a few moments to go into the sanctuary for conversation and prayer together?" They agreed. When we were in the beautiful sanctuary, Rudy sat about half way back, and I told her I would like to stand in the pulpit to get the feel from a preacher's viewpoint. As I stood there, I looked down at her in the empty church pews, and I said, "Honey, I don't think I'm ready for this."

As long as I live, her answer will be in my thoughts. She said, "Dick, I know we're very young for this assignment, but together, with God's help, we can do it." That was my Ruth.

It was a new start for her and a very great challenge for both of us. I could never adequately express my gratitude to the good people of that church for all their support in the many things we did during our five and a half years with them. There were a number of members of the church who were professors at Rutgers University, then a college for New Jersey women. There were three doctors in the congregation. That was very helpful because all three of our children were born at Middlesex Hospital in New Brunswick. The congregation also completely supported my development of a daily broadcast from the church over radio station WCTC. Even more, they were supportive of my furthering my education.

Before our children were born, we helped to house a blind couple for a little over a year. Also, even after Patty's birth, when Rutgers University was pleading for assistance by residents in the city housing university students, we opened the parsonage doors to two fine young men who ended up baby-sitting for us on Thursday nights when Rudy loved to go shopping. Even for years after their graduation, we heard from them once or twice a year. (I should have mentioned earlier that we always felt if we had room in the parsonage wherever we were, we should share when others who were in need. Even for the short time in our former parsonage in Atlantic Highlands we had housed a couple, Don and Ruby Giles, and their little son, Ira, who were involved in World War II at Fort Dix. They were from Cullman, Alabama.)

Because she was small, five feet tall, and weighed only ninety pounds, a doctor in our church prepared her for each of the births of our three children and was present for the deliveries. In her early pregnancy, Dr. Jack VanMater said, "I'm going to prescribe a careful diet because I want you and this baby to be strong and healthy." Happily, Ruth stayed healthy and active during each of her three pregnancies. She said, "As long as I can fit into the car, I want to go with you to any meetings and events to which you want to take me." During one of her pregnancies, we were at a large church gathering in Asbury Park. She started having contractions, and I took her to the local hospital, where they measured the timing of the contractions and said we could get back to our own hospital. Those were anxious miles, but we made it, and everything went fine for the birth of our first child, Patricia Louise. Even with our second child, Suzanne Gaie, Ruth still wanted to keep going as long as she could.

When the American Baptist Foreign Mission Board learned of our interest in missions and our serious preparation for an administrative position in a college, they interviewed us for the presidency of Central Philippine University on the island of Panay, Iloilo. Sponsored by the Foreign Mission Board, the university was already sizeable and somewhat of a flag ship in education. We looked over the assignment and discussed it with several influential members of the Board and decided we would accept. The Board acted positively, and we started the process of having all of the necessary prerequisites. All seemed to go well until we got to the health examination, when the doctor said, "I'm sorry to report that your wife and one of your children are anemic, and I know what the torrid climate is like in the Philippines because I was there during World War II, and I am not going to approve your going until this anemia is cleared. That will take at least a year." Needless to say, we were very disappointed. But not for long.

The needs at Alderson-Broaddus College were soon brought to our attention. The Reverend Lee Shane, pastor of Calvary Baptist Church in Charleston, suggested to the college trustees that they send several members to visit us in New Jersey, with the thought that we might be interested in coming to the presidency. Wayne Hawker, Chairman of the Board at A-B, and Dr. Asa Harris, on the staff of the West Virginia Baptist Convention, came to New Brunswick. The conversations went well, and our visitors seemed enthusiastic about recommending us. One of them said, "Reverend and Mrs. Shearer, you don't need to go to the Philippines to feel you are in mission work. Just come to us in Philippi." During Thanksgiving Week of 1950, we made our first trip into the heart of West Virginia and to the little town of Philippi. As we drove south through Grafton, with sixteen miles left to reach our destination, Ruth said, "We might as well turn and go back. I couldn't be happy here."

I remember her saying something like that when we were first married, and I answered, "Honey, we're not there yet. Before we decide, let's wait to see first-hand what the opportunity is."

Ruth always loved college campuses, and even though there wasn't much of a campus at that time, the challenge appealed to her as well as to me, and a bit later the trustees gave us a formal invitation to become president and First Lady of Alderson-Broaddus College. Ruth would be needed also in teaching as well as perhaps as Dean of Women. I was the youngest college president in the country at that time. I was probably also the lowest paid; my annual salary was $4,000. Rudy's, for teaching twelve credits and serving as Dean of Women, was $1,800. This truly was a mission and an adventure.

A LOOK BACK – FIFTY YEARS AGO: The Shearer children, Pat, Suzie, and Rick, join their father in fishing in the Atlantic Ocean east of the New York Harbor. The results in the catch of blue-fish are evident in the faces of the children and Dad. (See Dr. Shearer s column on page ____)

FISHING FROM THE **PATRICKSUE**
(L TO R: PAT, RICKY, SUZIE, RICHARD)

Setting Sail

THE LAST BAG WAS PACKED. It hadn't been easy to include everything, but I had often prided myself in a certain mechanical knack for getting the most into a small space. Ruth and I would be planning a lot of unusual vacations in the years ahead. She got most of the ideas for family changes and was a dynamo in caring for details in relation to the needs of our three small children. I often thought Ruth was like a tug boat pulling an ocean liner into dock – small but packing power enough to maneuver a job twenty times her weight and size. We had often witnessed such a navigation scene from Sandy Hook, N.J., as we looked across Raritan Bay. However, many of the organizational details of our travels were left up to me, and I assumed them gladly.

We were a happy family, but things had happened too fast during our marriage for us to be relaxed. Now, after five years of marriage, Rudy was working into the role of minister's wife quite well – although not in the traditional manner. She was too independent and effervescent to be subdued by any role, but she wasn't arrogant or aloof. As a child she had vowed never to marry a minister, but once she made her choice, she was determined to be the best minister's wife possible. I often claimed that my good fortune in finding such a capable wife was simply "dumb luck," but Ruth insisted, and with conviction in her tone, that her marital choice had been painstakingly deliberate and more like a "conversion experience" than anything previous in her life. She had prayed earnestly about the decision and told her father, when he questioned her decision, "Dad, I just know this is right for me."

Now it was 1950. We were the pastor and first lady of the First Baptist Church of New Brunswick, New Jersey. I skipped lightly up the porch steps with arms outstretched to help her with the baby. She commented on my boyish ways and said she was glad all over again that she had married Dick Shearer. Her family life and the work of the church had become a greater challenge than the summa cum laude honors she had won at college. Early teamwork had been difficult because we had both been like spirited horses pulling and prancing in our own arena. But we were learning the meaning of marriage and love, and we pulled the load of church and community leadership and family together in a fuller way each year.

We were happy in our work, but we could not help wondering what was in store for us. Where could our talents be best used? What were Ruth's ideas? I knew this vacation would be a time for "setting the sail" again—time for taking inventory—for reviewing the past and attempting to unlock the future. I remembered our first fishing trip in Raritan Bay when the fellow had steered the boat to find a specific fishing spot miles out in the bay by looking back and lining up a floating buoy with a certain building on the shoreline. Ruth and I would be doing some looking back as well as forward on this vacation.

"Let's get going. Vacation time's a-wasting," I called as I pushed hard on the trunk of the car to lock the lid in place. The two girls, Pat and Suzie, scurried into the back seat. Our six-month-old son, Ricky, was enjoying a new car seat sandwiched between his parents on the front seat.

The family car with the newly built boat trailing behind was an interesting sight to the neighbors on Livingston Avenue. We were overloaded. The children had insisted on taking most of their toys with them in the back seat. We intended to be away for around a month, but this was the same as a year in the quantity of clothes and volume of objects needed. The year before, the "Domine" had gotten the boating and fishing fever. Not that I spent much time at it, or ever would, but I usually became an enthusiast at whatever I undertook, and as a result had built a fifteen-foot outboard runabout which the whole family could enjoy. The family was skeptical whether or not it would float, but at least it served as a trailer for carrying all the excess household items which we could not get into the car.

The load had enlarged immensely because part this vacation was to be spent in renovating a third-floor apartment in an old house which we were purchasing on a monthly payment plan at 81Third Avenue, Atlantic Highlands. The owner, a widow by the name of Elizabeth Beckhorn, had reserved life tenure for herself in the use of the first floor and in income from the second floor. The Shearers were to pay a monthly amount as long as she lived. Then the house would be theirs. This arrangement was Miss Elizabeth's idea. She had no family of her own, so we had become close.

Added to the vacation items in the boat, therefore, were all the old furnishings we did not need at home but would need for the anticipated apartment—a small four-burner gas stove, several lamps with battered shades, a box full of old dishes, a rug left over from the last parsonage, several mattresses, odds and ends of curtains, draperies, and many little knick-knacks.

Given a little time, energy, and some help from me, Ruth would make that old attic into a penthouse retreat. I glowed over the fact that she could make a palace out of almost any hole in the wall. I had watched her do it before just by switching furniture and hangings and by adding carefully matched paint colors to cover up the opaque and the drab. But she always worked under stress. She could not unwind until things were orderly and tasteful. The first week would be hectic.

The car, trailer, and boat (officially named the PATRICKSUE for all three of the children) eased slowly out of the drive, down

Livingston Avenue, through the main part of town, and onto the highway east.

It was four o'clock before everything was unpacked. I wiped the sweat from my forehead and neck, glad the job was over for the time being. I knew that with Ruth, the job of moving furniture was never completely finished. The things which were immediately useable were in the attic where we intended to live (perhaps "exist" would be more accurate), and the long-range items were in the basement with a lot of other clutter. The girls were playing in the backyard with a friendly little dog, and Ricky was in a playpen nearby. Ruth was attempting to bring order out of chaos.

"Well, kids," I said, "tomorrow we'll launch PATRICKSUE and take her for a good spin.

We might even get in a little fishing."

"You'll have to take the first ride alone," said Pat suspiciously. They would have trusted Grandfather Shearer's construction, but Dad was new to this role, and there had been uncertainties as he put the boat together.

"She'll take it with the best of them," I bragged, "and you just watch her speed when we get beyond the harbor. That thirty-five-horsepower Johnson motor will make you think you're flying." Fortunately, the hull was a one-piece fiberglass product by the Goodyear Company, so essentially there was no danger even if the frame, fittings, and decks did not fit perfectly. But the job looked good, and I was proud.

Before ascending the stairs to the attic, I slowly walked around the house, surveying our first sizeable possession and calculating its needs and potential.

Ruth had had a dread of old houses. She liked things that were pretty and new, like the houses along Ocean Boulevard and down around Rumson and Deal, where we would often drive on Sunday afternoons. Her preference probably stemmed from impressions in her early life. Her family had always lived in industrial areas of Pittsburgh. Ruth had been born in the shadow of the Westinghouse Company. Later they moved to Connellsville, which was some relief, and still later to Weirton, where there were money, a progressive steel company, and friendliness, but always a lot of dirt in the air.

When we had contemplated the Atlantic Highlands purchase, I suggested that we could fix the attic into a summer retreat, and when Elizabeth Beckhorn was gone, we could rent out the first and second floors and practically make it pay for itself. Ruth finally went along with the idea but with tongue in cheek. Much would have to be done to the old house before it would satisfy the standards of even a not-too-fussy man, let alone Ruth. A paint job was needed badly. I could do it myself if I had a two-section ladder, but it would be better if I could get Dad Shearer involved with us during some summer vacation. The old cedar shingles had curled and were beyond paint or repair. I discovered that the shingles had been placed over lap-siding many years before. I hoped the siding would be good enough to be painted after the shingles had been removed. All of that must be <u>someday</u>. Just now I needed to get upstairs with the children and help Ruth arrange things for tonight.

"Why did we ever buy this old house?" she said tearfully. "I hate every inch of it. If you were the husband you ought to be, you would never think of bringing your wife and three children to a filthy, crowded place like this."

"Give it time," I begged. "The children look on it like camping and love it." I saw my attempt was in vain, so I changed the subject. "Why don't we go out for dinner, up to Matawan? We can afford that a few times while we're here. It will be easier to cook by tomorrow."

"You're a Pollyanna if I ever saw one." She simply had to voice her frustration. "Why don't you admit this was a bad deal? You'll put twice as much money in this house as it's worth, and what will you have in the end—an old <u>shack</u>! Why can't we have a decent house like everyone else?"

"Give it time," I said again, irked but trying to be casual.

"Don't try your smooth talk on me," she said. "Use it on the women of the church, but I'm wise to it. You're just not a business man, and you might as well admit it."

"There's a good fish place up the road." I tried to divert the conversation again. "And they have children's portions. If you are particularly sweet, I'll even get you a shrimp cocktail with sauce that will make your nose tingle." I squeezed her nose gently with my thumb and forefinger. She started smiling.

While she primped and got the baby ready, I fixed the girls and wrestled with a few mattresses in the front room, laying them on the floor where we would all be sleeping. I wasn't always patient with quick outbursts, but I was learning to understand them. When Ruth was tired, feelings were out and over. I did not get ruffled as easily, but I held ill feelings longer. I wondered if in the end her way was better. Everyone knew how she felt, and most times there was no lingering grievance. She stood in contrast to my mother, who was gentle and soft-spoken. As a tiny girl, Ruth had learned to speak out to be heard. She was proud and self-disciplined, decisive and analytical and always honest. I was sure the contrast between the two women was lessening as Ruth got older. They adored each other. I was learning what two different women were helping me to become – and I was thankful for both of them.

It was Saturday before we got around to launching PATRICKSUE. It had taken five days and nights of labor before Ruth would give in to a day off. Things on the third floor left much to be desired, but the miracle was beginning to happen. The day was perfect for the christening. Our oldest child, Pat, now five, helped wash the boat and put on the adjustable canvas canopy to protect the occupants in case of rain and to make the boat look more pretentious. Right now we all wanted beach and sun, water and more sun, fish and still more sun, and we knew just the place—the beaches of Sandy Hook. On the ocean side the fishing was usually good and one could get a spectacular view of lower Manhattan with its skyscrapers piercing the sky eleven miles away.

The harbor was just three blocks from our penthouse, but by the time the Shearers got to the launching pads, there were cars, trailers, and boats lined up for miles. The American flag and the harbor master's flag stood out firmly, blown by a brisk 15 MPH southwesterly wind. Large boats had docked at the Atlantic Highlands piers for the summer, and people were living in them as though they were living in sea-trailers.

Anxious fishermen had long since vanished beyond the seawall in an early morning search for fluke, porgies, bass, and blues. This multi-million dollar harbor had become Atlantic Highland's largest business, although the old town was no longer the summer resort for New York citizens that it had been many years ago. Pollution of the bay and the ease of transportation to southern Jersey had affected the habits of the vacationers.

"Get the baby and the bottle of ginger-ale, honey," Captain Dick said. "Girls, take the lunch and beach umbrella while I get PATRICKSUE backed into the water and unhitched." You might have thought I was in command of a thirty-foot Chris Craft. Men, women, and children were scurrying past us with bait, fishing rods, batteries, nets, and lunches. One group had already returned with a basketful of bluefish averaging three to five pounds.

"Stand back, girls, and let Daddy handle the car and boat," warned Ruth as she held Ricky in her arms. Back, back, back went the trailer, down the launching pad and into the water until the trailer was out of sight, with the boat resting on top of the water. I hopped out of the car and released the pin holding the motor, took the trailer rope out of the bow-hook, and brought the boat in for Pat and Suzie to hold until I got the car and trailer out of the way.

Finally finding a parking space, I loosened the battery from the car and took it to the boat. Someday I hoped we could splurge on a battery just for the boat, but already we had spent a tidy sum on the whole outfit. Then, with the battery attached to the lead wires and the gasoline tank pressure built up, all seemed in readiness. I stepped back to take charge of our son. "Before we get in, we must christen her, and that's Mother's privilege."

She came to the bow with the bottle of ginger-ale. "Here goes. I christen you PATRICKSUE," she said as she swung a mighty blow. "Here's hoping you hold us all safely." Ginger ale splattered over the boat and in Ruth's face. She had done the job well. The children laughed with glee but insisted Dad would have to get in first. We cleaned up the broken glass, and I hopped in, started the motor, whizzed out into the harbor, standing up and speeding more than the 10 MPH sign designated. Returning to the launching spot and loading the family and beach paraphernalia, I headed the boat out around the seawall and toward the beach four miles away.

We liked Sandy Hook because the beaches were government property, and since World War II, with the defense installations having been moved inland, families had been allowed to use them as long as they did not go into the interior of the peninsula. There was rumor that the government was going to open a federal park on part of the narrow strip. The tip of the Hook was a favorite spot for fluke fishing and also provided white sand. Usually we had occupancy almost to ourselves except for the fishermen and families who beached their boats while they had lunch. Because one of the deep channels came within several hundred yards from the end of the Hook, we would often get a very close view of large Esso or Mobil gas tankers going up the bay to unload at the Jersey refineries. A little further out, beyond Ambrose Light, was the main channel to the New York harbor. On several occasions we spotted the Queen Mary and the U.S.S. United States, but we could never remember which had two and which three smokestacks.

The tang of the salt air, the murmur of the waves gently splashing on the shore, the white boats dotting the blue water, the laughter of the children building make-believe cities in the sand, our love for each other, and, above all, our awareness of much that had been given in our young lives, made reflection and joy come easily. "If people could just relax and enjoy the world in which God placed them," I said, "this would be a much happier place."

"Oh, Dick, you always talk that way," Ruth said. "Maybe some people relax too much."

"I'm not a peace-of-mind philosopher altogether," I said. "In a world where evil is rampant, no God-fearing person can put his head in the sand. People should probably do what Jesus did. He engrossed himself in people's problems and needs but then got away to the desert to spend time alone. People are afraid to be alone today. They're afraid of their own thoughts."

"We don't have much time to think," she said. "You're in meetings every night, in graduate school two or three times a week, and always holding somebody's troubled hand." Her tone changed. "We're almost thirty years old. We have three children. We've each got one life to live, and nearly half of it is over already. I like New Brunswick and the church, and I'm proud of every inch of you. I believe we're loved by our congregation and respected in the city. You're getting more and more opportunities to serve on state boards and committees. I just want to be sure of one thing—what do you want to do for the rest of your life?"

I knew she could read me like a book, and this super-sensory perception often haunted me. I smiled. "I have been doing some thinking. We're a team, and I've been trying to think where our talents could be used best. I could not be happy thinking I had left behind this kind of service for the Lord. But what would you think of an educational job on the mission field?" She propped her head on her elbow, looking tiny and cute in her new red and white bathing suit. "You're a born teacher," I said. "Your years of high school teaching and the interim teaching you did recently in the Rumson Day School were challenging experiences. I enjoy the pastoral ministry, but I would also enjoy an administrative job in one of our Christian colleges on the mission field. I think I'm a good organizer, and people seem to respond well to my leadership–I don't mean to brag."

"You're judging yourself fairly," she said.

"I don't know if I could do it," I said, "but now that I have my master's degree, I might try for my doctorate. Columbia has an excellent program in college administration, the best in the country."

Her eyes brightened, "I've always wanted to be married to a man with a doctor's degree."

"We would not do it for status' sake." I said. "I couldn't be happy unless I was doing a job that many others might not be willing to do. That's the reason I mention missions."

"Where would we go?" Her mind was racing now. "Bermuda, Hawaii, Paris, London, Spain, Rome?" All those were places she had always wanted to visit, but the Baptists had no mission work of consequence in those tourist spots.

"We'd have to make contact with the mission board and find out what the needs are," I said. "American Baptists have schools in Burma, the Philippines, Japan, Africa, and I suppose many other places. It wouldn't be easy, but we might be able to make a contribution, and at the same time it would enrich our own lives."

"How long do you think it would take you to finish your doctorate?" She sat up to be sure the children were all in sight.

"More hours of course work," I said. "I'd have to arrange a conference with one of the professors in the higher education department." I was excited about the possibility and could tell she was, but there were many unknowns.

I scrambled up and ran toward the children, sweeping up baby Ricky and holding him high over my head. As I ran toward the waves I called back, "Last one in is a yellow-belly." Ruth and the girls scampered after me.

ONE OF OUR TRAVEL GROUPS
(RUTH FOURTH FROM RIGHT ON GANGPLANK)

Ruth Sparks Worldwide Travel and Lasting Friendships

"I WANT TO BE REMEMBERING and not wishing." This was the motivation and theme of much of the Shearer family travel. Ruth was determined to have us travel as a couple and as a family. She said, "I heard my mother often say that she wanted to go to Florida, but my parents never felt they could afford it. When we children got old enough to earn money and offer to send Mom and Dad, my mother was not physically able to go. I saw her often sitting on our front porch in a rocking chair, wishing she could travel. I determined at that time that I would do everything I could in my adult life to fulfill the dream of traveling, remembering rather than finding myself in a rocking chair just wishing."

One day when we were driving in the New York City area, she said, "Dick, we're going overseas soon." I chuckled, thinking we weren't yet financially able, but she continued. "Without your knowing it, I've been taking money out of your dresser drawer and saving it. I have also joined an educators' travel club at Columbia. They've made arrangements for a charter flight to London this summer at a bargain rate. Hopefully, we can become part of that group going to England and then have a month to travel around Europe, returning to London to head home. I thought after we discussed the trip, you would agree for Betty and

Billy to go with us." I reacted positively but also in shock, deeply appreciating the contacts she had made to make the trip possible. The Shaws, Ruth's sister and brother-in-law, were excited about the prospect. Ruth made the reservations with the club for the flight in a 99-passenger, four-motor Saturn airliner. (It was 1963, and jet engines were not yet in commercial use.) It was a long flight each way, and the plane rattled and was very noisy, but we got there and back without major problems. I made arrangements, once we got on the European continent, to rent a Volkswagen for most of the month, and I did the driving while Billy smoked his cigars in the back seat.

The rest of the story is history and is covered well by Ruth's journal. As she noted, we went from London to Paris, where we visited all of the usual tourist attractions—the Louvre, the Eiffel Tower, and so on. One of Rudy's comments is amusing: "Rooms in France generally have wash bowls and 'douche bowls'—quite a new item to us—while toilettes and bath tubs are rarely private. Toilet paper is furnished but very heavy, rough quality. Bed sheets also are of heavy, coarse material and are pulled over the pillows so as to avoid separate cases....The boys enjoyed the city latrines that are everywhere in Paris."She made special comment concerning having tea in a tenth-floor restaurant which offered a magnificent view of the city.

After Paris we visited several cities in Switzerland, primarily Zurich, which Ruth described as "truly beautiful." She mentioned the fact that the smell of Linden trees is pervasive, and we both enjoyed attending a women's Christian conference, with attendees from sixteen countries singing the Doxology in their own languages.

In another Swiss town, Interlachen, we stayed in a charming chalet, paying just $1.50 per night per couple. In Grendenwald we drove through the Alps and rode the longest chair lift in the world (7,000 feet) up the Jungfrau, which itself towers at 13,658 feet.

Italy came next in our itinerary. Our first stop was in Milan, where one night thieves broke into our car and stole not only the Shaws' suitcase containing clothing but also several valuable gifts and some jewelry and our camera and film. Then on through Verona to Venice, where Ruth and Betty particularly admired the Venetian glass on exhibit. As we left for Austria, Rudy wrote, "The gondolas are very colorful and the canal ride is quite picturesque. I'm glad I've seen it, but I'll have to confess that so far Italy would have to rate last on my list of favored European countries." I mildly disagreed, for I loved the statuary and other art and music in Florence and elsewhere. Ruth did add a modifier. "Music was everywhere throughout the piazza and the buildings of Italy are magnificent."

The Bavarian Alps and Tyrol country were breathtaking and took us to Innsbruck, beautiful in its setting and provider of excellent food, but expensive for housing and shopping, Betty and Ruth's favorite activity throughout the entire trip. Billy and I usually tagged along, but we occasionally side-tracked to go bowling or to explore a few back alleys.

Munich was highlighted by visits with our dear friend Ruth Tuttle and her husband and darling daughter. Then on to Salzburg, where we stayed in a pension for $2.40 per room—including the usual breakfast of coffee, rolls, and jelly. I spent a good deal of my time with Franz and Thelma Treml, friends of Ruth Tuttle's who eventually agreed to head up the A-B overseas program in Austria. All of us toured "old Salzburg," however, including the fortress and the cathedral, and the more we experienced of the city, the better we liked it, especially the Mozarteum and the cathedral and the Baptist church and its pastor and his wife. It seemed a far better center for the A-B students than Vienna or Munich might have been.

Holland was a special treat for Ruth. "From childhood," she wrote, "I have always been especially intrigued with Holland as I have pictured it from reading, and the windmills have always been symbolic....We did see some wooden shoes worn by people in a small village....One old Dutch man who was having a mid-day drink had left his crude wooden shoes at the door, and before he left he slipped them on, mounted his bike and was off. Another man on a bike with a small child was wearing a slightly fancier pair....The shoes were not pageantry."

On to Brussels and Luxembourg, where, after the women purchased Belgian lace and did more shopping in a flea market, we had to buy a large, inexpensive suitcase in which to carry our month's purchases. Ruth said, and then wrote in her journal, "I am determined next time not to buy trivia but to save my funds for larger works of art." Knowing her tendencies, I just smiled and nodded.

Traveling by train, boat, and air, and after touring London on our return trip—including dinner at the Café Royale, a treat provided by Billy and Betty—we were back in the United States on August 12, 1963—almost exactly fifty years before this memoir of mine is being written. Ruth's final journal comment was "The trip was indescribably meaningful and wonderful. We loved every minute of it, but we are happy to be home and to take up our active lives as citizens of the U.S.A. with new pride and appreciation."

This was the first overseas trip, just the beginning of our travels during our forty-eight years of marriage. We found a number of dear friends, both from Philippi and from the Board of Trustees and from other contacts in West Virginia, who liked to travel with us. We went twice around the world, twice to the Passion Play in Oberammergau, at least twice to Baptist World Alliance meetings, once in Tokyo and once in Stockholm.

It was while we were in Tokyo that one of my favorite incidents occurred. Other members of our travel groups always waited for Ruth to scout out the territory, to find the most intriguing souvenirs and to get the best prices. On this occasion, she was exploring the shops in the basement of our Tokyo hotel, and she came across a jewelry store displaying what looked like exceptionally beautiful, reasonably priced earrings and necklaces. While others of the women stood watching, she examined several pieces, told the clerk which she intended to purchase, and then said, "Some of my friends will probably also buy from you, but only if I am convinced that you are being honest. I want you to know that my brother-in-law is a judge back in the United States, and I will let him know if you cheat us. In other words, if you're lying to me about the value of this jewelry, you will suffer the consequences." Fortunately, all turned out well, with our companions convinced all over again that Rudy certainly knew how to shop.

We also went three times to Mexico City, trips made in our own little plane. A final commercially arranged family trip took us through the British Isles the year after I retired from the Alderson-Broaddus presidency.

Of all the places we went, all the cities we visited, Ruth always loved Pittsburgh the most. It was natural that she should feel this way, for she was born in the shadow of the Westinghouse Air Brake Company. The suburb in which she grew up, Wilmerding, where her father was pastor of the Methodist church, was some distance from the center of the city, and she often related how, as a family, the Mansbergers rode a bouncing trolley from their home into the city to shop.

The Rev. Dr. Arlie Mansberger was transferred from Wilmerding to the Central Methodist Church in Connellsville, and Ruth and I met in the high school there. He was later moved to the church in Weirton, with each move considered a larger parish with more responsibility. Even in Weirton, however, the family was within reach of Pittsburgh, and Rudy made the most of it, both by commuting for her graduate education and by joining a group of young, unmarried individuals for trips to the William Penn Hotel, which sponsored many entertainment activities including nationally known bands. Not all the church parishioners were sure the minister's daughter should be involved in such events, but Rudy always said, "What harm is there in it? I enjoy both the music and the dancing." Her activity along this line certainly paved the way for her to help in liberalizing the social life on the Alderson-Broaddus campus.

Her love of the city was evident when we were deciding on positions at that college. Ruth made a bargain, saying, "I'll agree provided that we go to Pittsburgh at least once a month and New York once a year." We didn't make it that often, but we did cover the roads to Pittsburgh quite often.

The trip that is uppermost in my memory happened on a tragic night many years after we had come to Philippi. Over the years the Benedum Foundation had been a major support for most of the private schools in West Virginia. Michael Late Benedum, a native son of Bridgeport, had become a highly successful oil wildcatter in various parts of the States and in other countries, and he was very generous with Alderson-Broaddus.

I will always remember the visit Dr. Hu Myers and I made to see Benedum and his sister, Sophie, who was still living in Bridgeport. The relationship between brother and sister was a joy to behold. Sophie had bought a new hat and put it on at a daring angle. Coming into the living room to show it off to the three of us, she spoke directly to her brother. "How do you like my new fedora, Mike?"

He quickly responded, "Sophie! You look like a trollop."

She snapped back, "How do you know what a trollop looks like?" We all laughed.

A codicil to his will reveals what a balanced Christian and business life Mike Benedum lived.

The story of this Pittsburgh relationship does not end happily, however. The vice president and chief legal counsel of the Benedum Foundation was David Johnson, another native of Bridgeport. David's chief office assistant was lovely Nancy Arnold. Together they made the offices in the Benedum-Trees building on Fourth Avenue in Pittsburgh a home away from home for any of the college presidents who visited. If Mike himself was there, he would always invite us to be his guests for lunch at the Duquesne Club, where he had a reserved table. I'm sure this was a highlight of all the schedules that we private college presidents experienced while we were fund-raising. The entire region has sorely missed one of its greatest sons since Mike Benedum passed away in 1959.

After years of warm fellowship with David and Nancy, and at least two million dollars in Benedum gifts to A-B, Ruth and I received a call one evening from David saying, "I need your help even tonight. Nancy Arnold has passed away, and I am to go to the funeral parlor to see her. I don't want to go alone. Please come to go with me."

We put everything else aside, dressed quickly, and left for Pittsburgh. When we reached his apartment we found that David himself had suffered a heart attack and had been taken to Presbyterian Hospital. We rushed there, only to find that he had died. We were asked to identify the body, which we did. Neither David nor Nancy had children, and we felt a great deal of responsibility for making contacts. I phoned the chairman of the Benedum board, who lived in suburban Pittsburgh, and he said, "Please help me make arrangements." We were all in shock but managed to maintain enough balance to make plans to lay our friends to rest.

As we later drove toward home that traumatic evening, I was speeding a little in Greene County, just north of the West Virginia line. To our shock, a patrolman flashed his lights and sounded his siren behind us. I pulled off of the highway, and the police officer, whose name I learned later was William Kersicki, flashed a light in my face. I briefly told him what we had just experienced and said that we needed to get home as quickly as possible.

I had heard stories that Greene County patrolmen were particularly interested in West Virginia vehicles, but this was my first encounter with such. I said, "Please, just give me the ticket.

I know I was speeding, but I need to get home to contact other people about the two deaths we have just experienced."

His attitude was anything but understanding. He said, "You're going to sit there until I read everything on this ticket."

I said, "No, I'm not. Give me the ticket and I'll pay the fine, but I'm going to be on my way."

He got very angry and threw the ticket at me. I pulled out, only to find him following, then pulling ahead to demand my stopping again. Even though it was midnight or after, he demanded that we follow him to see the Justice of the Peace. He led us across the river, into another county, and got a Justice of the Peace out of bed, and Kersicki read us the riot act. It was three o'clock in the morning before we got home from that fateful trip to Pittsburgh.

In the morning Ruth, who had suffered through the entire incident with me, asked what I was going to do. I said, "You know, I think that traffic officer went way beyond his rights, and I think I will call my Waynesburg cousin and see if I can bring some kind of action to teach the officer a lesson." We soon had a court proceeding in Waynesburg with Officer Kersicki there, and the judge's decision was to give the officer a reprimand, and I was ordered to pay the fine, which I had agreed to do from the beginning.

That episode resulted in one interesting and positive event. Months later one of the college vans got stopped in Greene County by, lo and behold, William Kersicki. When he saw the name of the college on side of the van, he smiled at the driver and said, "Your president doesn't think much of me, and I want to show him that I still have a heart. You were speeding, but I'll just give you a warning this time." When the students got home they thanked me.

Around and around the world, back and forth in the United States, and now content in Belvista, my home near the college, my life is still very full, not of wishing but of remembering.

A Visit from Brother Howard
(l to r: Howard, Ruth, Richard)

An Angel on My Shoulder

It was my brother, Howard, who coined the phrase to describe several life-threatening experiences which I managed to survive without a scratch. Two of these incidents involved flying, the others non-flying.

I would never advise any of my friends to learn to fly the way I did. I don't mean that the flying decision was wrong—very much the opposite. I think it was one of the best decisions I ever made, both in terms of my work as college president and in terms of my family. However, my caution for others regards the method and the equipment with which I started.

Wilbur Simpson was teaching several World War II GIs to fly at his family farm with its 1500 ft. runway located in the country halfway between Philippi and Belington. After I had traveled 20,000 miles by car throughout much of West Virginia, which in the '50s a and early '60s had no interstates, I finally said to Ruth, "If we're going to stay with this job, I've got to find some other way to get around. I think I'll try private flying."

She laughed and said, "Yes, you and the birds."

I said in return, "Honey, I'm serious."

I went to talk to Wilbur, asking if he would take me up for a brief flight. I had been in a small plane only once before, during a Fourth of July celebration near Connellsville. The flight with

Wilbur in a Piper Cub was brief. As we landed in a cross-wind and experienced several bumps in landing, I said to myself, "This is not for me," but my second thought and determination was "Others can do it, and so can I."

Wilbur said if I owned my own plane, he would teach me for a hundred dollars. After examining the list of used airplanes that were listed in *Trade-a-Plane*, I decided to borrow $900 from my father and bought a little two-seater, 90-horsepower Ercoupe.

That type of plane helped to revolutionize private flying, but it was not good for cross-country aviation. It contained only one radio in the dashboard, with tubes performing the transmission. Transistor transmission had not been invented yet.

Also my Ercoupe did not have a cockpit starter but instead had to be started by manually "propping" the propeller from the outside. I did this for several weeks successfully, but one day when I was in a hurry, I got inside the plane, adjusted the choke and throttle quickly, and, standing in front of the plane, began to prop the motor. Suddenly, I realized I had left the throttle full power. The plane leaped forward, with me jumping out of the way just in time.

As the plane accelerated, I grabbed the right wing tip, holding on with all my might, with the plane going in circles and gaining speed. I yelled to the farmhand standing within sight, begging him to grab the other wing. Instead of attempting any interception, he ran the other way. It was a good thing he did!

There we were, the plane full-throttle, going in circles, with my limited ability to hold it much longer. I could see the plane going down the runway, climbing into the air without a pilot, doomed for destruction, only the Lord knew where. I can't give a final answer as to how the next few moments happened, but above all, I think there was an angel on my shoulder, guiding both my thoughts and actions. I let the plane go at precisely the right moment and allowed it to crash into the hanger doors, where Wilbur had two other planes housed. The corrugated steel doors tore up the wood propeller and stopped the engine. I was an emotional wreck but safe on the ground.

When Wilbur came running, he assessed the situation and was very helpful in his comments. He said, "Dr. Shearer, you did the best thing. I'm not sure quite how you gauged when to let go in order to have this best possibility happen. The doors can be repaired, but you'll need to buy a new propeller, and the engine will need to be magmafluxed, but you're in one piece, and the plane is repairable."

Another incident happened even closer to home. After we had purchased a ninety-acre farm from Lester and Ruth Holbert, I developed an interest in raising cattle. Al Shroath, a Christian businessman with an automobile dealership in Clarksburg, found out about our acquisition and he said, "You've got to get something grazing on the land or it will simply grow up and give you trouble." He further said, "I have a heifer left from a sale of cattle on my farm in Ohio, and I will give it to you if you'd like to start a herd." His suggestion was generous and made sense, so I gratefully accepted.

The herd grew to thirty cows and one bull. Each summer, with the help of John Mayle and a few of my family members, we made three thousand rectangular bales of hay, storing them in the upper part of our barn and a hay shed. I know some folk questioned whether the college president ought to be involved in cattle-raising, but I enjoyed the animals and found it a way of reflecting my upbringing and also felt that in our location in Barbour County, it gave me acceptance by the many local farmers. They enjoyed advising the college president as to how to help a cow give birth to a calf and how to accomplish many other tricks of the trade that they had learned years before I came on the scene. I also felt that during the late '60s, the cows helped to keep me sane when there was a great deal of student unrest throughout the country. We didn't have much at A-B, but the atmosphere on our hilltop was affected to a small degree.

My pride and joy in the farming routine was my Massey-Ferguson tractor. It was a beautiful red machine which I secured in the early '60s. It helped me keep the land around our home bush-hogged and beautiful.

On this particular day, I was bush-hogging in the field next to a neighbor's farm boundary. A creek ran along the roadway at the bottom of a steep field, and a small bridge had been built to allow access across the stream and back onto the main road. The weeds and grass had grown around the bridge so that I couldn't see the sides. I wanted to cut as much of the growth as possible, and I got off one side of the bridge with the back tire of the tractor. This made me lose control of the steering, and the tractor ran severely to the left and down into the creek next to the neighbors' fence. When I got off the tractor and surveyed the situation, I knew I was a very fortunate man. I could not see how that tractor kept from turning over, with me under it. I paused and said a prayer of thanksgiving to the Good Lord. I got another farmer to come with his tractor to pull the Massey-Ferguson out of the creek.

Three other life-threatening events are worth mentioning briefly.

Many of my fellow presidents had had automobile accidents as they drove many miles over West Virginia. For instance, Duane Hurley of Salem College had had such an accident in Charleston. I was always grateful that I had escaped over many years, but one day I was late because of having made too many phone calls back in Philippi. I was on my way to the office of the Foundation of Independent Colleges, then housed in the Security Building in Charleston. It was nearly lunchtime when I reached mid-way near Flatwoods. I decided to stop at Sutton to see a friend who had always been a generous donor to the Foundation. I was traveling at least sixty miles an hour but began blinking with sleepiness. All of a sudden, immediately in front of me was one of the huge direction signals that state road workers use to divert traffic. I couldn't stop, so swerved but hit the sign broadside with the passenger side of my Chevrolet sedan. Fortunately, my car did not cross the median into the lane of oncoming vehicles. I got out unhurt.

A number of state road workers came running, and when they saw what had happened, they asked how they could help. "This is not reportable. No one else is involved, and you're o.k." They arranged to have my car taken to a garage in Sutton and found a way for me to proceed to Charleston.

I realized again that an angel had been on my shoulder. At first I wasn't sure why the DOH men had acted so helpful, but on reflection I learned that the heavy iron directional sign should have been at the side of the road, not in the traffic lane. I did not make an issue of it, just remained grateful for my safe escape.

Another life-threatening incident happened when I was flying to Lewisburg in my AeroCommander 400J. I had already taken and passed the course in instrument flying at Cleveland Hopkins Airport and, fortunately, had enough instruments in the plane to feel comfortable in making instrument landings. My friend Angelo Koukoulis at the Clarksburg airport said that he had breathed a sigh of relief when I got my instrument rating because he knew I would be able to fly much more safely than before.

As I followed the "landing plate" into the Lewisburg airport, I got the ILS frequency, turned the proper knobs, and lessened the speed to ninety miles an hour. At first I leaned back, feeling confident that this would take me in safely. However, I soon sensed that something wasn't working correctly. As I looked at my compass, it was not agreeing with what the ILS required. I quickly lowered my speed to eighty miles an hour and started looking for land under the haze. I finally came out of the bad weather, only to note that I was off course by at least a thousand feet. I had a ceiling of only three hundred feet. I saw the airport approximately a thousand feet to the left. I jerked the aelerons, banking the plane sharply to the left. The man in the tower realized that something was wrong and said that I should circle and try again. I made a quick judgment that I could land on the long runway, perhaps the longest in West Virginia. I did that, using every foot of the latter half of the runway.

Naturally, I went to talk with the man in the tower, who of course wanted to talk to me. After parking the plane, I ascended the tower and was glad to find the man friendly instead of hostile. His first comment was "That was a good landing."

I felt some shock but managed to communicate decently. "What in the world was wrong? My ILS would not lock in to yours."

He said, "What frequency were you using?"

I reported the landing plate data, and he said, "We changed that frequency a month or so ago."

I commented that my landing plate did not have the new frequency, and I made no more of the issue because I knew it was my responsibility to keep abreast of the changes, but I said under my breath, "I wish controllers would announce it for a month or so when a new frequency is installed." I went on to my meetings at the Greenbrier, knowing that my brother was right when he said I had an angel on my shoulder. I said a prayer of gratitude later that night.

The most dangerous situation of all occurred in 2007. I had begun losing my eyesight. My regular ophthalmologist, Dr. Farris in Bridgeport, had removed a cataract from one of my eyes, but this was a new problem. After full examination, he said, "There's something else wrong that I can't fully analyze. You need to go to a specialist."

I hired Megan Schulz, a Physician Assistant student and manager of my nearby Hillcrest Apartments, to take me around the state to find a doctor who could help correct my deteriorating situation.

Megan was working both as the manager of my apartment building and also at Rite-Aid drugstore, but when she agreed to my request, she made a comment I will never forget. "I will put your needs first." This she did. We went to a doctor in Clarksburg, then to one in Buckhannon, then three others. In a conversation with my friends at Poling's Store one day, Peggy Poling and her mother suggested that I go to Dr. Dunderville, who was a specialist in treating swelling around the retina in the back of the eye, which the other ophthalmologists had diagnosed as my problem.

Megan took me to him in Parkersburg a number of times, and he tried several possible solutions, finally saying I would need at least seven injections over an eighteen-month period. For a while my eyesight improved, and we were all hopeful.

Megan was unable to transport me for the final treatment, so my son-in-law, Dr. Terry Jones, came from Huntington. I needed some gas put in a barrel to use in the tractor which we used to clear the fields, so we put the barrel on the back of my truck, planning to stop in Clarksburg, where the price of the gas was significantly cheaper than it was in Philippi. We drove to Parkersburg, the sky clear, the temperature in the nineties, and saw the doctor, with the truck sitting out in the sun.

On the way home, we stopped at Quiet Dell to fill the barrel with some fifty gallons of gas. Terry got out to pump the gas while I sat in the truck to try to recover from the seventh injection and my disappointment at having had Dr. Dunderville say, "I thought we were making progress, but the swelling has returned, and I've done all I can."

Terry had half-filled the hot barrel when I heard him yell. I looked out and saw flames. He rushed to fill a bucket with water and started splashing the fire, but to no avail.

There was just one other customer at the tanks. He saw our dilemma and quickly pulled the floor mat from in front of his driver's seat and ran to help, yelling, "You have to smother it." He did that, and the flames went out. He said that the hot barrel had caused the problem and that if enough oxygen had gotten to the gas, the entire area could have blown up. He ran back to his car, and Terry hurried to thank him and offered to pay him. He said no, that he was happy to have been of help.

We drove home still fearful of an explosion. Fortunately, we made it safely, putting the truck in a shady place. We waited for the barrel to cool off before we made another move.

Terry and I both knew we had had an angel on our shoulders that day. That one man had been present and had known how to handle the problem. Hesitant to tell the details to our family until much later, we said an extra prayer of thanks that night.

RICHARD IN HIS FIRST PLANE, AN ERCOUPE

GOING MY WAY?

WHENEVER I WAS PLANNING A trip and had empty seats, I offered a ride to anyone going in my direction. Sometimes that was a bit risky, but it always worked out without serious consequences. A good example has already been described, the trip to Mexico when Ruth and I had Marie Raebold as a companion. On another occasion, I carried three passengers. Barbara Smith remembers that experience.

"It was far smaller than Air Force One, and there were fewer passengers and many fewer bells and whistles. And, obviously, it was a different president, but it was a president's plane, a Tri-Pacer that belonged to Richard Shearer, president of Alderson-Broaddus College, where I had been teaching for some nine months.

"It was his generous idea—my hitching a ride from West Virginia to Wisconsin to visit my parents. He and a member of the staff of the West Virginia Baptist Convention were to attend a meeting at the American Baptist conference center near Green Lake, Wisconsin, and they would be glad to drop us—me and my eighteen-month-old daughter—at a small airport where my father would meet the entourage.

"Wanting to impress my boss and that other guy whose name I have forgotten, I had decided to wear a black-and-white print dress and shiny new black patent leather sandals. Jean, my gorgeous child, was equally well dressed.

"Into the air we went, over northwestern West Virginia,

southern Ohio, northern Indiana, around the tip of Lake Michigan, and up past Chicago to the postage-stamp air field west of Milwaukee. Fine weather, fine company, fine take-off, fine air currents, fine landing. I couldn't wait to share Jean with her grandparents.

"We taxied up near the cracker-box-sized terminal. Dr. Shearer shut off the engine but stayed in his pilot's seat. The other passenger, whose name has still not come to me, needed to use the restroom, so he climbed out of the plane, took two steps on the friction strip that edged the top of the Tri-Pacer's wing, and jumped down onto the tarmac. Then he turned to help me.

"Thank goodness I handed the helpless infant to the nameless man, for seconds later, as I began to disembark, my foot slipped off the friction strip, and I fell off the wing of the plane.

"To make a long, painful, story short—my dad came to get me and my baby. Dr. Shearer and his colleague headed on for their meetings. I spent the next month black and blue from the top of my head to the soles of my feet.

"How's that for the distinction of being the only person ever to fall from the president's plane?"

Don Smith also flew with me several times, the most memorable trip being one to celebrate the seventieth birthday of Senator Jennings Randolph. Here is Don's version of the story.

"Working at the time as Assistant to the President at Alderson-Broaddus, I was invited to join him in what proved to be a dramatic trip to Washington, D.C., to attend the 75th birthday celebration for U.S. Senator Jennings Randolph.

"Nudging the throttle forward, my take-off from the Barbour County Regional Airport went smoothly. President Shearer often allowed me to handle the controls because I had flown with him many times and had completed ground school at Benedum Airport.

"We flew into one of Washington's small airports and hitched a ride to the nation's capital. I remember the long lines waiting to congratulate the senator, and I'll never forget the buffet tables full of gourmet foods, especially a huge pile of chilled shrimp—a tremendous treat for me and apparently for a middle-aged woman who filled her plate, then stepped out of line to let others pass and returned to visit the shrimp two more times.

"When the party was over we headed for home, but this time the flight was considerably more challenging for both the pilot and the plane. We flew into thunder and lightning over the Shenandoah Valley. By the time we crossed the Alleghenies, I thought we might be close to clipping the tops of the trees on Spruce Knob. I was holding onto the control panel because the plane was being tossed helter-skelter by the storm.

"That's when the lightning struck. I quickly let go when I felt the shock of electricity coming through the panel. The single-engine propeller became a circle of light, the wings and the instruments engulfed in a bright glow.

"As we approached Philippi the storm subsided, but we were faced with a new dilemma—a thick fog had enveloped the area, and we couldn't see the ground.

"Following his instruments, the president flew in circles over Philippi until, miracle of miracles, we saw the yellow lights illuminating the Sentinel Coal Mine near Corders Crossing. With this orientation we lined up with the runway and, just in time, caught sight of the airport landing lights. With a few bumps, and buffeted by gusts of wind, we were on the ground—a flight I will never forget."

I always thanked the Good Lord for every trip that ended without my having to use the insurance policy which I carried to cover my passengers.

RUTH NAMED WEST VIRGINIA MOTHER OF THE YEAR 1974

OUR LITTLE GIANT HAS FALLEN

RUTH HAD STRONG CONVICTIONS CONCERNING end of her life. She had a detailed and prophetic vision of how she would die. Fortunately, it did not cloud the wonderful contributions she made as a wife, a mother, a professor, and a friend to many. However, she shared this peculiar prophecy with me and the children, even with her sisters, Betty Shaw and Vivian Tarr, on a number of occasions. She said, "You watch and see. I will have a bad fall, and if that happens and I lose capability, please don't try to keep me alive by heroic means. I do not want to live without full mental capacity. Just let me go to be with my Lord."

Her earthly years concluded almost as she had surmised.

We were in the interim pastorate of the Bridgeport Baptist Church. Since retiring after thirty-five years at Alderson-Broaddus, she had been commuting for four years to West Virginia Wesleyan College to teach in their education department.

A couple in the church choir had gotten married, and we had scheduled a dinner at Minard's restaurant for the choir to honor the newlyweds. A married couple from the New York/Connecticut area were living in our trailer at the time—Guy and Martha Turtoro. Guy was at A-B in the Physician Assistant program, and Martha, who already had a college degree, had secured a teaching position in the Taylor County school system.

They were a delightful couple and participated in the Bridgeport church by singing in the choir. Martha even sang solos once in a while. We had taken them with us to the celebration dinner that fateful night and had come back to Philippi together.

We all unloaded, and Rudy started up the stairs to the first floor of our home. The Turtoros headed for their home on a knoll just above our house. I walked to the basement door to turn on an outside light so that they could see their way up the hill, then waited for them to be out of sight so that I could turn out the light.

I glanced at Rudy as she climbed the basement stairs. She was carrying nothing but a small purse, and there was a railing for support. She was almost to the top when I saw her lose her balance. She managed to pass the little landing, but as she attempted the last three stairs, she fell completely backward, hitting her head on the basement floor.

I called for the Turtoros to come to help me. We carried her to the car and took her to Broaddus Hospital, where Dr. Karl Myers met us in the Emergency Room. When he saw what had happened, he said, "We've got to get her to a neurosurgeon, and the closest one is at United Hospital Center in Clarksburg." The ambulance was called, and she was transported there as we followed in my car. The neurosurgeon met us at UHC. After a thorough examination, he said he would operate the next day.

It seemed like everything went according to expectations, and on Monday Rudy seemed to be close to being herself again. We were very hopeful of her full recovery.

Such was not the case. She lapsed into a coma, and even though she opened her eyes at times, she never regained her health. The doctor suggested that we read to her, pray with her, talk to her, sing to her and remind her of happy family incidents, all to excite her mind.

I was extremely grateful for the help of the church. I took the morning shift, and they arranged to have various members be with her afternoons and evenings. We were still hoping and praying for a miracle.

Her fall had occurred on November 3, 1992. During the Christmas season that year, her brother, Arlie Mansberger, who was a medical doctor in Augusta, Georgia, came. He met with the neurosurgeon and another UHC doctor. Together they determined that we had lost Ruth in November. There was nothing more that could be done.

My brother Howard interpreted her death in a way that I and all three of our children and her sisters appreciated. He said, "Our little giant has fallen."

Her memorial service in Wilcox Chapel at the college was a great victory salute to both her and to her Lord and Savior. Our hearts are still in pieces, but we celebrate the life, God's gift to us, of Ruth Mansberger Shearer. With the support of the Scripture, I believe that she will rise again, and we will someday be reunited.

RIDING HIGH
(L TO R: RICKY, PAT, SUZIE C1951)

THE NEXT GENERATION

ANOTHER FIRST LADY AND SCHOLAR

WHILE WE WERE AT THE New Brunswick church, Church World Service was concerned about displaced persons who didn't want to return to their own countries where Communism was entrenched. After screening applicants who wanted help, CWS contacted various American denominational headquarters, and requests went out to individual churches to sponsor refugees, helping them to find housing and employment. Our congregation accepted responsibility for the Usenko family, refugees from The Ukraine. The family consisted of an older father and mother, their daughter and her husband and two children, plus a second daughter with one child and a husband. We managed to find housing for the older couple and the first daughter and her family but not for the second daughter and family. We Shearers felt called to share the parsonage with them.

Even though she was hardly older than they, our first-born, Patricia Louise, developed a strong, motherly instinct for the Usenko children. For the older children who were ready for elementary school, she insisted on taking them. We lived on Handy Street, near the New Brunswick firehouse and close to Livingston Avenue, a main artery out of the city. Our church was located just a few blocks from the parsonage, and so were a couple of public schools. Our Patty would escort the little Usenko children, which meant crossing wide Livingston Avenue. Sometimes there was a safety officer to give them permission to cross, but that was not always the case, and when they had to do it on their own, it was a risky business. One day when Patty came home, she ran upstairs and crawled under the bed. We knew something was wrong, but it was quite a while before she would come out and tell us. We learned later that she had just narrowly escaped being hit by a car. I insisted on taking her and the other children to the crosswalk to be sure an officer was on duty. Otherwise, I would lead them across myself.

Soon after we had moved to Philippi and Alderson-Broaddus, when Pat was six years old, we found her putting pennies—her "allowance"—into a piggy bank. When asked why she was saving them in that way, she replied, "I want to help A-B get back on her feet." This act was a good indicator of two of Pat's strongest characteristics—loyalty and determination.

As Pat was growing up, she always had a favorite phrase that she would say to me as we were preparing for evening prayers. I remind her of it to this day when she telephones. That phrase was, "Daddy, I love you whole bushels." She knew she was loved whole bushels back.

The marching band and the football games at Philippi High School and later at Philip Barbour High School, were always central in the extra-curricular activities for many of those attending. This strong emphasis impacted our children. Pat became a baton twirler and a majorette with the band. In addition, she developed contact with a dozen or so younger students who wanted to learn the skill of baton-twirling, so she took them on and had a class which met regularly. I can still see her on the large lawn close to Greystone, the president's home, teaching her class. Ruth and I had hoped that all of our children would take piano lessons and even learn to sing, but for Pat, the emphasis was too strong in the marching band direction.

As Pat got ready for college, and this is true of Suzanne and Rick as well, Ruth and I counseled with them, suggesting that they go away for at least one year. As parents, we thought learning to handle the problems as well as the joys of independence are part of growing up. Accordingly, all our children left for a year or more, with Pat doing all of her college studies away from A-B. Because of a mutual tuition agreement and a deep relationship with other colleges, there were a number of schools where our children could get tuition benefits. Ottawa University, was the strongest Baptist-related school and had an excellent academic program. Even though it was far away in Kansas, Pat enrolled there.

Our family will always remember the trip we made to take her to Ottawa for her freshman year. We loaded the plane and left with our full load from the Clarksburg airport. Our flight path took us around Chicago, and by that time I knew we needed to refuel. I had landed once at O'Hare, but it is such a busy airport that they prefer not to have general planes stop there. Meigs Field, no longer in existence, was in the downtown area and was intended for general aviation planes and was my favorite small airport in that area. However, Midway was also appropriate and was located south of the city. I made contact with their tower and landed there, pulling up on the tarmac where I had been directed. As we unloaded briefly, we noticed thousands of people pressing against the pedestrian fence in anticipation of a great event. A large private jet landed and pulled up right beside us. The door opened, and the stairway descended, and out bounced The Beatles, obviously what the crowd had been looking for, and there we were, right next to them. Somewhere we have colored slides of their arrival, but of course, the celebrities soon disappeared with their security guards into the crowd. The Shearer children still talk about that incident to this day. The first trip to Ottawa was memorable!

Pat loved Ottawa but said she missed the mountains. They

were building a dormitory near where she was living on campus, and she said that on many mornings, she would look out her window and see a pile of dirt near the excavations. This reminded her of the West Virginia hills and of the east.

By this time Art and Peg Brandon, graduates of Alderson-Broaddus in the 1920s were very successful leaders in higher education, he having held the position of vice president of the University of Michigan and, later vice president of New York University. Art had grown up in Belington here in Barbour County, the son of a Baptist minister, so they visited us whenever they came back. We also visited them in Michigan and in Weehawken, New Jersey. For a while, the Brandons were also deeply involved with Bucknell University. When they heard that Pat wanted to come back to the mountains, they encouraged her to check on Bucknell. She visited them in Lewiston and decided to finish her college degree there. For those two years the Brandons, who had retired, with Art now a member of the Board of Trustees at Bucknell, lived close by and served as Pat's surrogate parents. During her final years at Bucknell, Pat got to know an A-B student, Richard Wilson, from Point Pleasant. He visited her at Bucknell and won her heart. After they both graduated, Pat reported that Dick had proposed and she had accepted. I said, "I think you have good judgment, and I like Dick." After marrying, they both completed their doctoral degrees and have spent many years in higher education. They are presently finishing their tenth year in the presidency at Illinois Wesleyan University in Bloomington, Illinois. They have two children, Adam and Rachel, and five grandchildren. Although all of them have been miles away from their home base at Philippi, the lines of communication and love remain strong.

When Pat and I were in a serious conversation concerning her future and her upcoming marriage, she said, "Dad, there are very few Dick Wilsons left in the world." That was good enough for me, and the years since then have proven that her evaluation of Dick was accurate. They have made an outstanding team in educational leadership, even as I think her mother and I were as she was growing up.

I could not be more proud of my first child and older daughter, and I am deeply grateful for her constant communications and her frequent sacrificial trips to Belvista for a visit and to offer valuable insight and advice. She and Dick and their two children and their grandchildren bring joy to me and to all with whom they come into contact.

OUR OTHER LITTLE GIANT

Another little giant grew up among us. My good friend Blaine Corder said to me in church one Sunday, "I wish I had a daughter like your Suzie." He knew of her frequent three-hour drive each way from Huntington to Philippi to be with her dad. He knew, too, of the caring relationship she built far past our family, especially with her husband Terry's family and even beyond.

I said, "I wish every parent had a Suzie. I love my other two children no less, but because she is the one living the closest, it has fallen to her to look after me." I also have mentioned Suzie's many talents, including being a fine mother of three children, Derek, Chase, and Allison. Several of Suzie's talents have developed in recent years and include her ability to take responsibility for managing the eight apartments in the building I own above the college tennis courts. I have seen her handle the problems of renters graciously, kindly, and yet firmly.

She also thrills me on each of her visits with her musical ability, playing on the piano many of the sacred songs I used to sing while in seminary and during my years in church and college work. Every night when she is with me, a little before nine o'clock, she helps me get ready for bed, then goes to the piano to give me a half-hour concert of these pieces that still mean so much to me, like "The Lord's Prayer," "The Stranger of Galilee,"

"I Walked Today Where Jesus Walked," and "Bless this House." As she plays, I mouth the words, remembering almost all of them. We end with a good-night kiss, and I fall blissfully to sleep.

When Suzie was just a toddler, Ruth and I often traveled. Suzie would stay with my parents at their home in Connellsville, and when we would return from being overseas with a tour group and would call to tell my parents that we were coming to retrieve Suzie, my mother would always reply, "Suzie is very happy here. We love her. Please let her stay a little longer." We sensed that our parents considered her something of a "God-send" to help replace the nine-year-old daughter they had lost many years ago—Ila Merlene. She had died suddenly of meningitis in the early 1920s. She was my only sister and took care of me as the baby of the family.

While we were living in Greystone on the Alderson-Broaddus campus and while Suzie was still in elementary school, Leonard LoBello was hired as our business manager. We knew he had a heart of gold, and we also knew he had the ability to say no, a trait which I always said was a requirement for his position as well as my own. This was particularly true as we attempted to add buildings, to pay decent faculty wages, and at the same time to balance the books. However, sometimes this task made people feel he was a little gruff in his responses and interactions with them.

When Ruth heard that his wife, who was a prominent member of several regional psychology organizations, would be away for a week, she told him she would prepare dinner for him. When the meal was ready, Suzie was asked to be the courier. He came to the door, and she said, "Mr. LoBello, my mother sent this."

He answered, "I told your mother I didn't want anything. I can cook for myself."

Little Suzie hesitated a moment and then said, "Mr. LoBello, take it and be grateful."

What made this a positive experience was that Leonard often

told the story himself and laughed about it. We had all learned that Suzie could stand her ground when necessary.

In these later year as our family has faced different needs and we have loved, encouraged, and supported each other, this has become a family motto with one thing I added: Accept, Adjust, and Be Grateful.

Suzie and Terry met at Philip Barbour High School, and both Suzie and her husband, Terry Jones, graduated from Alderson-Broaddus College. During their junior year at A-B, they both went with our study group to Austria. In order to raise the money for Terry's expenses, they went door to door on campus, selling personal items they could do without. On one stop they offered the Don Smiths a record player which Don graciously purchased for $30.00. Terry also sold pizza from the local Dairy King in the dormitories, and I always felt this was an early indication of their determination to work together and find a way to earn their way in life.

After graduation from Alderson-Broaddus, Terry and Suzie were married and Terry earned his doctorate from the School of Dentistry at West Virginia University. Suzie hs her master's degree from WVU.

Both Terry and Suzie stayed close to me as I developed health problems, which seemed to hit a high in the years following 2007, when I began losing my eyesight. In particular, Suzie made a visit when I was struggling and had just gotten out of the hospital. When Suzie saw my condition, she phoned the doctor directly and pleaded for attention. Dr. Holbert saw us that very afternoon. I fainted in his office, and he found that my sugar count was very low. As I came to, he was feeding me a candy bar. He and I both gave Suzie credit for saving my life.

I agreed with my brother Howard as he referred to my wife Ruth in her latter years as "our little giant," but when we lost Ruth, we gained another little giant in Suzie. I suppose this characterization would never more evident than during the serious illness and death of her husband, Dr. Terry.

He had been physically fit all of his life, having been a wrestler in high school and at Alderson-Broaddus. My friend Dr. Bob Digman tells of having watched Terry wrestle when his opponent had Terry's arm in almost a breaking position, but Terry would not give in. That was his kind of determination all through his life.

Suzie was a cheerleader in the same high school class, and they were voted best school spirit, most dependable, and cutest couple. Instead of working toward material goals alone, they dedicated their professional lives to serving others, Terry as a dentist in Kenova, WV, and then with the Department of Defense in Germany and the VA in Huntington, and Suzie, for over twenty years, as a social worker and case manager with Health South Hospital in Huntington, helping stroke victims and their families.

Unfortunately, Terry's health took a serious downturn in 2012, and when he was examined thoroughly, it was determined that cancer had spread throughout his body. Suzie took off from her work and for three months was with Terry day and night in the hospital, with their children and his brothers providing relief. When my grandson Chase called me with the sad final news, he said simply, "Grandpa, my father is gone."

I remembered Ruth's fall in November of 1992 and her death. I fully believed in what Jesus said: "I go to prepare a place for you, and if I go, I will come again and receive you unto myself, that where I am, there you may be also. Peace I leave with you. My peace I give unto you, not as the world giveth. Neither let your heart be troubled. Neither let it be afraid." In spite of this assurance, I completely withdrew for almost a month. I couldn't even answer the telephone without breaking down, and I certainly couldn't carry on my preaching at the Bridgeport Baptist Church. As I thought back on my reaction to the loss of my Ruth, I marveled at Suzie's reaction in the loss of Terry. She participated in a beautiful graveside service on a windy day on the Corley Methodist Church hillside outside of Philippi. On the following Sunday, a celebration of life service was held for Terry at the Kenova Baptist Church.

My other children commented on the strong testimony Suzie gave—a wonderful tribute to her husband and to his life and their faith in the Lord. At both services their children also shared personal stories of their care and love for their father and family. Their pastor, The Reverend Steve Willis, and The Reverend Bert Coffman, a longtime friend and high school classmate, led the services, but all present felt strengthened by the heartfelt sharing and powerful witness of the Jones family's personal walk and journey through life and Terry's illness. Suzie, Terry, and their family have blessed us all. Their children and Chase and Alana's two sons, Miles and Shade, have been a delight to them both. Suzie has returned to work, and her children and grandchildren will continue to fill her life with joy. We are excited that their daughter, Allison, and her husband Andrew, will welcome a baby boy next year—their first child.

I am happy that Suzie and I have many week ends together. I look forward to her visits, her piano concerts, and the spiritual bond that strongly unites us.

Accept, Adjust and Be Grateful
Always believing in a good
And faithful God and HIS grace.

OUR BEST MISTAKE

"I am very proud to announce that my father, Richard Shearer, will be ringing the closing bell on Wall Street this afternoon at 4:00 pm. EST. With hard work and the help of a great team,

Emerge Energy Services has gone public and is making its mark on the New York Stock Exchange, with 60% growth from its opening day price, proof that hard work, vision, persistence and sacrifice pay off, and it's never over unless you decide to give up."

Paul Shearer, my grandson, wrote these words this past week about his dad and my son, Richard "Rick" J. Shearer.

On August 27, 2013, Rick and the company he and his team built from scratch rang the closing bell on Wall Street. I think it must have been satisfying and rewarding for all the hard work and dedication that Rick exhibited in every endeavor he ever undertook. Yes, if I could describe my son, the words that come to mind are "the hardest worker, the most loyal, the fully committed."

Rick has enjoyed a successful business career. He was in New York City at 270 Park Avenue by the time he was 27 years old. He and his wife, Candy, moved to Connecticut fresh and green from the hills of West Virginia. He was a young manager with Union Carbide. I can remember well visiting them. Rick took me up to his office on the 37th floor, and I remember him looking out the window at the tall skyscrapers, saying, "Wow, Dad, sometimes I can't believe I really work here."

Not that he didn't have his share of ups and downs in the business world. There were disappointments along with the triumphs, as there are in most endeavors that are worthwhile. But all in all, it seemed to come together as Rick himself said, "as if it were perfectly planned." He told me recently that he had thought about every job he ever had, ones he liked and ones that he did not. It seemed they all had served a purpose. He thought seriously about them, from his first job out of college working in the WV Soil Conservation Service in Barbour County right up until he found himself as CEO of Emerge Energy Services. Every position seemed to prepare him for the day he stood on the dais of the NYSE watching the company he had built go public.

Rick was born in New Brunswick, New Jersey, on August

22, 1950. His mother was RH negative and during those days it was a risk for the mother and the baby. We had our two daughters but had wanted to have one more child. After all the warnings, we had a healthy baby boy, and Rudy did fine. She often said about Rick, "He was the best mistake I ever made."

I would say the first thing my son threw himself into was basketball. Growing up on the college campus, no doubt, was a huge influence as he would attend the games with us and watch the players practicing in the gym. Maybe he wasn't a natural, but he worked harder than most. He ended up being the all-conference starting guard on his high school team and on through his four years as captain of his team at Alderson-Broaddus College. I admit his mother and I worried about his focus on sports. We didn't want him to forget his academics. But he seemed to find a good balance. One of his greatest attributes was that he was able to transfer that hard work and dedication to his career.

A fond memory for me was when Rick invited me to fly up to Nova Scotia with him when he was working as president of a Canadian mining company. It was nice to have someone else making the travel plans, as I had always been the one planning for others. I enjoyed the opportunity to watch Rick deal with issues and to listen to how he handled the problems.

It was a beautiful part of the country, and we ended our visit with a fabulous lobster dinner with some of his business acquaintances. I have to say I added some drama on our way home as I began to feel lightheaded when we were in the security line at the airport. We ended up spending the day in a Canadian hospital, but it turned out fine. I truly enjoyed getting to be with him and seeing exactly what he was doing for a living.

By his side at the Wall Street ringing of the bell and throughout his life has been his wife, Candy, a loyal, supportive wife and mother. Candy and Rick met in junior high school and became high school sweethearts. Candy has deep roots in Barbour County and has often had to "keep the home fires burning" while Rick traveled with career needs. Candy has been a true partner as she has moved to different parts of the country and away from her own family as Rick's career opportunities required. She has also been a true asset to Rick as a trusted sounding board with important decisions in their home and work life.

Rick and Candy have two sons, Ricky and Paul, and two daughters-in-law. Paul and Celeste have one daughter, Presley Anne, and Ricky and Suzanne have just presented their parents with a grandson, Theodore Richard "Teddy." Rick and Candy are thoroughly enjoying their new role as grandparents.

A BRIGHT FUTURE
(L TO R: SUZIE, PAT, RICKY C1960)

Some Memorable Experiences and a Few Bits of Philosophy

My Only Deep Regret

Our strong friendship with the late Senator Robert Byrd developed over many years . When we first came to the presidency at Alderson-Broaddus College, Bob Byrd was running for his first political office. As he traveled around the state, and because he had no money to pay for motels or hotels, he was driving a station wagon in the back of which he had made a sleeping arrangement. However, there were times when he called on friends, including Ruth and me, for overnight lodging and breakfast. We were always happy to oblige and believed him to be a good representative of West Virginia in Washington, even though we didn't agree with him on all of his political stands. In addition to his visits in our home, even after we left the college presidency and I was serving as Executive Director of the Foundation for Independent Colleges of West Virginia, we kept in touch. I knew of his upbringing in Sophie and of his active membership in the Crab Orchard Baptist Church, where my good friend Dr. Shirley Donnally was minister, so I invited Senator Byrd to preach at the closing worship service of our annual meeting at the Greenbrier. He accepted and did a fine job.

The event that I regret happened one week end while I was interim pastor of the Bridgeport Baptist Church. I had contacted Senator Byrd's office and suggested that if the senator was ever in the Clarksburg area on a week end and would like to have an opportunity to preach, we would be glad to have him come to the church.

It was on a Thursday when I got a call from his office, saying that he would be in our area on the week end and would be available to us. I corralled several members to make telephone calls to insure good attendance. We also placed articles in the Clarksburg newspaper, which gave the story headline attention.

The church was full that Sunday. We even opened the Sunday school rooms for the overflow crowd. The people present already knew a great deal about the senator, so, wanting to say something different, I decided to use a story that I had heard somewhere. I said, "We're pleased to have our friend, Senator Byrd, as our preacher this morning. We all know that Bob was raised in Sophie and that he was brought up to love the Lord and the church, and we're glad that he represents many of the values most of us stand for. There is one incident in his early life that I'd like to share along that line. His father operated a general store in Sophie, where almost every need of the community was provided for. One day his father said to Bob, 'I have work to do in the storeroom, and I'd like you to manage the counter for the afternoon. I have just one request. Have a scripture in mind when you make a sale.' Bob agreed to the terms and took over. Several customers came, and he took care of their needs. One lady said she wanted to buy fabric for a dress. She asked Bob to show her appropriate material. Bob brought out a bolt of fabric and she said she liked the pattern. 'How much is it?' she asked.

Bob told her three dollars a yard. She responded that she wanted better quality. Bob brought out bolt after bolt, but nothing pleased the woman. Finally he brought the last bolt, but that still didn't please her. Once again she said, 'Don't you have anything else to show me?' Bob, not wanting to be defeated, and because he had spent a good deal of time with the woman, decided to bring out the first bolt again. Of course, she had forgotten having seen it earlier. 'I like that pattern,' she said. 'How much is it?"

'Six dollars a yard,' he said. 'Fine,' the woman said. 'Give me five yards.'

"The cloth was cut and wrapped, and she left happy. However, Bob's dad had been close enough to hear the conversation. He came out and said, 'Son, what scripture did you have in mind when you made that sale?' Bob answered, 'She was a stranger and I took her in.' Bob's dad laughed and said, 'Son, you'll go far in life.'"

The church audience laughed heartily and applauded for so long that I wasn't able to give my concluding line. Bob rose and stuttered a little more than usual as he started his sermon. "Oh, they tell all sorts of stories about me, but you can't believe them all."

What I had wanted to say was, "Now we all know our West Virginia senator has become in many ways the conscience of the Senate, and we're proud of that fact." I have always regretted not having given these important words. I wrote him a letter of apology. Later, when I saw him in Washington, I apologized in person. He brushed off the incident, but I still regret that event.

A Visit to Haiti and to the Mellons

I'm not exactly sure how we first made contact with Larry and Gwen Mellon in Deschapelle, Haiti, but the trip was memorable, with a number of points of human philosophy highlighted through the encounter.

Like most members of the Mellon family, Larry graduated from an Ivy League college—Princeton—, expecting to join the family in the banking business in Pittsburgh. He did this for a number of years but never felt satisfied that he was living the life he should be. After he met Gwen and they were married, they decided on a different lifestyle. They knew of Albert Schweitzer in Africa, and the more they read about him, the more intrigued they were to get acquainted with him and his ministry among the poor. Schweitzer had turned down a musical career and instead became a medical doctor and found a life of service in the heart of Africa. When he learned of the Mellons, he invited them to come to see his work first-hand. They did this, with the result that a similar ministry was what they felt called to establish. The path ahead would not be easy, but they were determined to prepare well and then enter a life of service.

Larry and Gwen both went to Tulane University, where he obtained a medical degree and she earned a degree in medical technology. Then they took a million dollars of their own money and searched for a destitute location in the western hemisphere where they would build a hospital and where their services would count. They chose the location of Deschapelles in Haiti, below Port au Prince and Cape Haitian.

We learned that they needed nurses at their new hospital, and since we had a strong nursing program at Alderson-Broaddus, we thought we might enter into a relationship that would provide education for some Haitian young people. Some of our students and graduates could also be challenged to work at the hospital, which the Mellons named for Albert Schweitzer.

The Mellons sent a driver to pick up Ruth and me at the Port au Prince airport. They were gracious hosts, and Ruth, because she had been born in the shadow of the Westinghouse plant in a suburb of Pittsburgh, related easily to many of their Pittsburgh stories. We saw long lines of folk wanting help with various illnesses, and we knew that the load was great, the problems extensive. Larry took me with him, walking through what at first seemed like a country village, but as we kept walking, hundreds of little mud huts appeared, where the tenants were trying to eke out an existence. They were sleeping on their floors, exposed to various rampant diseases. Dr. Mellon sometimes went out to see patients in their own huts. However, his main work was in the hospital and involved surgery and serious medical treatment.

I will never forget several things he said, such as, "Gwen and I came here to do just one thing—to heal as many people of as many diseases as we could. We soon learned, however, that that wasn't enough. We had to find out what was causing the diseases. One of the things we discovered immediately was that their wells were built so that rain water could run in, bringing all sorts of bacteria with it. We hired an engineer from the States to teach the people how to put collars on their wells. However," he said, "even that wasn't enough for us to include in our ministry." He continued. "One day several parents and other adults brought a teen-aged girl to the hospital on a stretcher. She had burns all over her body, and we didn't know whether she would live. No one would tell us what had happened. We gave her the best care we could, with the result that months later she recovered enough to tell us her story. 'I got sick,' she said, 'and I'm not sure what sickness it was, but my parents took me to a voodoo priest. He took me inside his tent and told me to undress. He poured kerosene over my body, then lit several candles and was going through his gyrations when one of the candles got too close to me, and I lit up like a torch. If it has not been for my parents and several other adults rushing in and smothering the fire, I would have burned to death.'"

Dr. Mellon said that they found that they had to help the people of Haiti understand what God is truly like. To help with this side of their ministry, they hired a Protestant minister to come to work with them and to provide Bible classes and worship services.

Ever since that visit, I have felt more and more how imperative it is to try to understand who God is. Although I know that this Haiti situation is an extreme example, it is a real one. Just believing that all concepts of God should be accepted as legitimate and logical is not very firm thinking.

Our college entered into a nursing exchange with them soon after our visit. Ruth Tuttle from Alderson-Broaddus went to work there, and a Miss Jerome came to A-B for her nursing education. I hoped that this would be only the beginning of a lasting relationship, but our nursing administrators thought there were scheduling problems that could not be resolved. This I still regret, but the impact of getting to know the Mellons surely blessed Ruth and me.

Larry and Gwen Mellon have died, but their work is carried on at the Albert Schweitzer Hospital in Deschapelles, and I believe that an active group in Pittsburgh still supports this worthy ministry.

DEALING WITH RACIAL MATTERS

My attitude toward other races was molded very early in my life. While I was still in elementary school, my father took me to several KKK meetings held on the school grounds in Poplar Grove, where I was born. Those brief experiences started out to be quite positive in that they encouraged patriotism and strong loyalty to our country. However, when the meetings and the KKK symbols started turning the interpretation of Americanism into something just for Caucasians and became negative toward those of other colors and backgrounds, my father stopped attending and shared his broader feelings about America. He did this more by action than by precept. For instance, he and my brother helped a black lady, Mrs. Washington, repair her house. He often led singing at the Swaggertown church, where most blacks attended. This provided opportunity for me to preach during my college vacations and on numerous other occasions. That little church was full most of the Sundays when I was present, and I enjoyed their enthusiastic reactions, which occurred even during my sermons. Because the atmosphere was informal and in order to give my sermons more liveliness than I would in my home church (First Baptist Church on South Pittsburgh Street in Connellsville), I would remove my dress coat while I preached. On one Sunday, a lady in the back row in the Swaggertown church stood up while I was speaking, lifted her arms heavenward, and called out, "Him telling the truth! Him telling the truth!" My whole background was one of inclusiveness and appreciation for the variety of responses received in different racial contexts.

When we moved to Philippi in 1951, there were a number of "White Trade Only" signs in store windows on Main Street, a characteristic of many small towns around America at that time. In order not to embarrass the store owners, we did not make an issue of the matter, but we were happy when in the early '60s, Martin Luther King, Jr., who was a graduate of an American Baptist college, Morehouse in Georgia, and an American Baptist seminary, Crozer in Chester, Pennsylvania, led the way in a significant turn-around in America. I wanted our work at the college to be part of that revolution, but we needed to do it peacefully. In an attempt to begin such a change, we honored several outstanding African-American leaders such as Jackie Robinson. He came to campus at our invitation for an assembly program. Marian Anderson came and received an honorary degree from A-B. Both of these "stars" made a lasting and forcefully good impression on our faculty and students. I wanted very much for Marian Anderson to sing for us, but I did not want to have her feel we were imposing. Hence, she came, was well received, and showed appreciation and kindness to all.

It was in 1963 that the first African-Americans were added to the Alderson-Broaddus faculty. Bruce and Tommi Redd, from Wilcoe and Boomer in southern West Virginia, were finishing graduate degrees at West Virginia University when they were hired. Moving to the A-B campus, they shared a duplex house with fellow faculty members Don and Barbara Smith. On Thursday nights, Barbara reports, Don would go to the Redds' half of the house to watch the TV show *The Rat Patrol* with Bruce, and Tommi would help Barbara with the three Smith babies while they watched *Dr. Kildare*. The Redds both completed doctoral degrees at WVU and gained wide respect in their teaching field, biology, with Dr. Tommi being named Outstanding College Teacher of West Virginia. Bruce died of cancer in 1996, and Tommi died of a cerebral aneurism about a year later. The science building on campus bears their name along with that of the Kemper brothers, alumni from Colorado.

Early in the '60s we had a brief student demonstration in the plaza behind Old Main, led by some of our black students who were joined by a few colleagues. Gary White, a prominent soccer player from Trenton, New Jersey, was one of the leaders. As I headed toward my office, he and some others stood on the steps of the building and said, "President Shearer, we're demonstrating."

After thinking for a moment, I replied, "I have work to do that I can do in the library, I'll set up shop there temporarily. I would like a small committee to come to tell me what this is all about. I will be glad to listen." During the next several hours, faculty members talked with the students, and the demonstration disbanded.

Later, some of the leadership told me, "We didn't have any issue against the college. A fellow from Fairmont came to Whitescarver, our dorm, several times, insisting that we were working against our race by not demonstrating. He made us believe that it was our duty to do so, whether we had a good reason or not." I tried to be understanding and even sympathetic.

Slowly, the "White Trade Only" signs disappeared, but several students came to see me with a specific grievance. "President Shearer, we are going to demonstrate downtown. We can't get our hair cut." I asked whether the barbers had been talked to, but the answer was that they had not. I explained that I was opposed to demonstrations unless they were absolutely necessary. Often they made more enemies than friends.

Hence, I said, "I'll go down with several of you to find out what the barbers actually think."

We went first to the barbers on South Main Street. We asked the two men how they felt about cutting the hair of our black students. Their reaction was extremely negative. They said, particularly to me, "You folk up on the hill try to tell us what to do, and we don't like it. Go back where you belong." We knew we had no chance there, so we left.

There were two other barbers in town. "Sleepy" Bryan had a shop on South Main, so we stopped to talk with him. His conclusion was, "I don't own the shop, so I can't make the policies, but I'll stay after hours and cut the hair of black students." We liked his attitude.

There was one final barber. He had a new shop in North Philippi and was anxious for college business. He said he would be glad to cut the hair of any student or faculty member. We left that last interview satisfied. Although the total attitude downtown was not perfect, the students could be cared for adequately, and we avoided the demonstration.

I enjoy greeting alumni when they come back to campus. Some take the time to stop by to say hello. Gary White, who has his own business now in Philadelphia and has been serving on the A-B Board of Trustees, is one of those who visits briefly. We hug each other, recalling pleasant years when he was a good student and an outstanding athlete. Recently, I remembered another fine student from my hometown of Connellsville, Cynthia Cole. She distinguished herself as a student, and I asked her to assist me in the teaching of a speech class. I knew she would play a leadership role in education when she graduated. Her story is a great joy to me, shared in a written statement she prepared at my request.

I felt that our job at Alderson-Broaddus was to spot and

develop and reward goodness and greatness wherever it existed, regardless of racial background. That attitude still exists at A-B.

THE USENKO FAMILY: FIFTY YEARS OF GRATITUDE

BROADENING THE HORIZON

One of our goals as we came to the presidency of the college was to experience the world and give opportunity for students, faculty, and local citizens to join in that experience. Even before that, however, we had a first-hand encounter with international relationships. This involved the Usenko family from the Ukraine while I was pastor of the First Baptist Church of New Brunswick, New Jersey.

The Usenkos, coming from Europe after the end of World War II, were part of large groups of displaced persons who did not want to return to their homes under Communist rule. The control in those countries was much more severe than most of us Americans realized. Church World Service, an international Christian agency, screened hundreds of these displaced persons and recommended them to the American churches for sponsorship. Our church agreed to adopt the Usenko family. We knew there would be seven people including an elderly parent couple, a son and his wife and child, and a daughter and her husband. We were told that only the daughter could speak English. Our responsibility as a church was to find housing for the entire family and employment for the two young men. The older father was beyond working age.

Mr. Edgar Vliet, Chairman of the Board of Deacons, and I drove two cars to the New York harbor, where we were told the ship had docked. We were amazed at the sight of the shipload of hundreds of refugees. Most of these people had all of their possessions in burlap bags thrown over their shoulders. Their only clothes were the ones they were wearing. It took us quite a while to find the Usenkos, and when we did, we were surprised to see that they were carrying a box about the size of a cedar chest. The daughter who could speak English was not with the rest of the family, but we managed to let them know we were their sponsors and would take them to their new home in New Brunswick.

We got them all loaded in the two cars and proceeded, having secured housing for the elderly couple in a duplex not far from the church. The young family was to live in the other apartment in the building. We had prepared a room in the upstairs of the parsonage on Handy Street for the son-in-law and the daughter, the latter of whom arrived on a later ship.

I was very grateful that we had several top-flight business CEOs in our church. One of them, Mr. Robert Humphries, who was in charge of the General Motors plant in Rahway, immediately offered the two men jobs.

As for the contents of the box which had been brought all the way to the United States, they gladly opened it, and I was happy to see three things: tools to allow them to make a living as carpenters; family photos (I was pleased that they considered families as precious in their lives); and several musical instruments (another indication of the quality of life they were seeking and the kinds of things they would enjoy).

In addition to caring for this fine family, we were busy with a growing church, a daily radio show for shut-ins named "Just What the Doctor Ordered," and for five years I traveled two or three afternoons a week by Pennsylvania Railroad to New York for my master's and then doctoral work at Teachers College, Columbia University. On top of all this, all three of our children were born during this five-and-a-half-year pastorate in New Brunswick. Ruth handled the needs of the children and the functions of a minister's wife with grace and effectiveness.

Our emphasis on trying to bring the world view to our work at the college in Philippi was pinpointed when Rudy and I in 1968-69 led thirty-three students in their off-campus semester in Austria. Several faculty couples preceded us in this travel to other cultures, but Ruth and I wanted to go ourselves, both for the experience and to evaluate the program. Dr. Franz and Thelma Treml were educators in the Salzburg area, and we hired them to guide and teach in the program.

We found that Europeans enjoyed winter more than do most Americans. Because of this, the opportunities for winter sports were easily available around Salzburg. We visited Hitler's old hang-out at Berchtesgarden in the mountains, a half-hour or so by bus from Salzburg. We got permission for our student group to learn to ski and to use both the lower and intermediate slopes. The cost was a dollar, including the skiing equipment, plus an additional dollar for use of the advanced slope. The Reverend Bill Bathman, pastor of the Baptist church in Salzburg, and his wife took special interest and were able to teach skiing to many of our group, including me.

I mentioned to the Bathmans that we needed an accomplished

pianist to teach at the college, and we were willing to sponsor that person. Europe, known for all its wonderful composers and musicians over the years, and where music and flowers were held in high regard, was, I believed, a good place to search for such a teacher. The Bathmans recommended that we contact Pastor Solc, pastor of the First Baptist Church of Prague. By phone he told us that he had a young lady immediately in mind. We set a date to travel to Prague where we could meet both the minister and the young woman.

Ruth and I drove to Prague, arriving in the late afternoon. We searched for a place to stay and a restaurant where we could eat, the latter being on the second floor of the hotel. We went in to find something on the table that reminded us both of America and of Ruth's hometown, Pittsburgh,—a bottle of Heinz catsup. Because we were there the night before the scheduled meeting, we checked on what was going on in the famous Dvorak Hall. To our pleasure, we found members of the music faculty of the University of Prague were going to be giving a concert. It was an enjoyable evening, and we were certain we had made a good decision in seeking a European piano teacher.

We found Pastor Solc's home late the next morning and discovered that he was quite Americanized, having spent some of the war years in the United States teaching tennis in several locations. Later, several of his sons came to American colleges and universities and won a number of tennis awards.

Just before lunchtime, Marija Sommerova arrived by train and joined us to eat and to talk about whether she would be interested in teaching at our college. Her husband, George, was not with her, but she assured us that he would like to see them together on a campus in America. We heard her play well and were glad for her limited ability in English.

At our invitation, they came to West Virginia, and although the adjustments to college work and to the little town of Philippi were not easy, they persisted. As the prime minister of Germany said once, "It's not enough for folk to emigrate. They must also be assimilated." George and Marija did well at the college for forty years, even sponsoring members of their family to emigrate as well. George became the college electrical engineer. In 2013 they retired to warm and sunny Florida. In their time with us, they certainly broadened the horizons of students, faculty, and local citizens of Philippi. I have always been grateful for the appreciation they showed to Ruth and me for sponsoring them and providing the careers they enjoyed at the college. It was a win-win situation. Even before they left West Virginia for Naples, Florida, they made time to visit me and to express once again their appreciation.

The same was true of the Usenko family. Even though we left the New Brunswick area a few months after they arrived in New York, they surprised us approximately fifty years later. Seventeen members of the family traveled a thousand miles round-trip to come to Philippi to tell us how much it had meant to them to become citizens of the United States and to have me, as pastor, and the congregation in New Brunswick as sponsors. Most of the young Usenkos have graduated from college. One even married the Director of Admissions at Rutgers University. The older men started a construction company and have done very well there in New Jersey. Their coming so far to say thank you will also remain a highlight in my life.

WHY DID YOU STAY SO LONG?

I was asked that question often toward the end of my thirty-three years in the college presidency. Somewhat jokingly, I would answer, "There was so much to do, and I was a slow worker." Usually my answer would bring a chuckle, and the subject would be dropped, but there was truth in both aspects of my answer. .

"There was so much to do." That was certainly evident to everyone who knew anything about the college. The best years of the school had been in the 1920s, when Elkanah Hulley was president and, yes, there was a football team and an athletic program with Art Brandon in charge. The new athletic building, which was later turned into space for the Social Sciences and Humanities, rightly named Withers-Brandon Hall, came into existence, not without financial danger and heartache. In the 1920s there was effort on the part of American Baptists to raise significant sums for their related colleges and their mission programs. On the intentions of this effort, Alderson-Broaddus spent several hundred thousand dollars to build the new gym. However, the campaign result fell far short of its goals, and all of the funds raised were allocated to missions. The college was left in debt and closed its doors in the late 1930s, and the campus was sold to a few investors. Fortunately, a few leaders in the Philippi community, many of them members of the Kiwanis Club, raised $30,000 and bought the school back. A member of my New Brunswick church had traveled through this area and, because of his knowledge of the financial and academic threats facing the college, advised Ruth and me not to accept the presidency. We knew it would be a big job to rebuild the institution, but we felt called to the college as a mission.

In the second place, my being "a slow worker," was in some ways untrue. I traveled by car and then by private plane, doubling the efforts of most college presidents. Two illustrations of my fund-raising technique are in order. First, Marie Raebold of Huntington had earmarked for the college over a hundred thousand dollars left to her by her husband. However, because she had somehow been mistreated, she was angry and had decided otherwise.

I knew I had to help her change her mind. I found out that she wanted to go to Mexico, and Ruth and I had planned such a trip for a vacation, so, with Rudy's approval, I invited Marie to go along. The invitation was risky, but Ruth agreed with the idea. The trip went well, and when we built Wilcox Chapel in the late 1970s, Marie gave $135,000 to establish music department facilities in that magnificent building.

A second example lies in the relationship between Ruth and me and Ruth Woods Dayton. She and her husband, Arthur, were natives of Barbour County and members of two outstanding Civil-War-period families. Arthur and Ruth had moved to Charleston and maintained a summer home in Lewisburg while Arthur served as legal counsel of a prestigious Charleston company. Arthur died before we could know him, but we became acquainted with Ruth while she was living in the Lewisburg home. I tried to present to her the needs of the college and my hope for a resurrection of that institution. Fortunately, there were already some signs of her interest in this. She said, "Richard, how can I give to Alderson-Broaddus? My father was chairman of the Board of Trustees at Wesleyan, and they expect help from me. I am a Presbyterian, and Davis & Elkins Collge expects my support. Also, we have a college right here in Lewisburg, and they expect local people to be helpful. How can I single out A-B?"

I said, in what I believe was a humble way, "Ruth, I can't tell you what to give or where to give it, but I would like you to consider one factor. Alderson-Broaddus is in the poorest county of any college in the state. There are many good people there, as you know, but little business or industry or wealth. Please ponder that thought as you consider your gifts."

It took us eight years to gain her confidence. Every summer she would make a trip to campus unannounced to check on how we had used her gift that year. She had had bad experiences with other gifts and wanted to be sure we were good stewards. Her first gift was to refurbish the guest room in Old Main Hall. The second gift was a Steinway grand piano, which we needed for the music department. She also gave $30,000 and portraits of her parents for the expansion of Pickett Library.

On one trip she drove to Greystone in her pink Cadillac and found my Ruth on her knees scrubbing the porch. Because it was hay-making time, I was in the fields several miles away. Rudy apologized for her appearance and welcomed her, sending a messenger to get me.

Two of Ruth Dayton's special gestures meant more than dollars to us. She put me on the Board of Directors for the Dayton Art Gallery in Lewisburg, an association which I greatly enjoyed. Also, one day when I was visiting, she said, "Richard, I would be willing to give you the lot next to my house if you and Ruth would build a house and come to live here." She even had plans for a house that she thought would look good there, one of the loveliest spots in the city. She also indicated that she would help us with the cost. When I shared this with my Ruth, we were both overwhelmed with gratitude but realized that we still had work to do at Alderson-Broaddus. We had to turn down the offer, but I did everything I could to show our appreciation.

As Ruth Dayton aged and became more dependent, we tried to stay close, even though we were more than a hundred miles away. Twice when I knew she was unable to go to the grocery store, I purchased several bags of groceries, put them in my plane, flew to the Fairlea airport, and, after knocking on the kitchen door and running away in order not to embarrass her, I left the groceries. I wanted to be helpful and not just a money-raiser. I'm sure she knew the source of her bounty.

In her estate she left a large amount of money to the Dayton Foundation. A-B received $30,000 annually for many years. She also left the college parcels of land and mineral rights in three counties. Recently the college president, Richard Creehan, told me a gas drilling company had surveyed all the mineral rights owned by the college. Those donated by the Daytons were valued at $5,000,000. He indicated that the company was currently unable to buy the rights but that the value was secure.

The college owes great appreciation to Arthur and Ruth Dayton.

Yes, I was a slow worker.

A Year of Sad Travel

Soon after I left the presidency of Alderson-Broaddus, I became interested in the subject of transitions, specifically presidential transitions. Ruth and I bought Continental Airlines senior passes and traveled nearly twelve thousand miles interviewing other presidents who had recently retired from college leadership.

One of our early visits was with a friend who had been a long-time and very effective president in a college in the midwest. He had built that institution to the point of high respect as truly Baptist-related and having a quality academic program. We found our friend living in the president's home on the fringe of the campus. The trustees had given him the house as a farewell present after twenty years of service. He was gracious but did not reveal the "inside story" of his retirement. His successor had tried to make a "little Harvard of the Midwest" out of the school and overshot in many ways, losing the distinct character of the previous institution. The college went through many changes of leadership in subsequent years. We were later sure that the ex-president died a heartsick man. The Board of Trustees recovered some ground, but they have never been able to relive the glory days of the '50s and '60s.

Another visit was with Harry Dillon, past president of Linfield College in McMinnville, Oregon. His wife felt that they had become somewhat isolated from college activities, but Harry was philosophical about it. They were living comfortably, still involved in some community activities, glad to be free of some of their previous responsibilities. The college was still progressing.

Verda and George Armacost were two of the most capable people in the entire American Baptist Convention. Financial stability increased during their tenure at the University of Redlands, as did academic standing. They were both in leadership roles in national organizations both academic and religious. During their last weeks at Redlands, the trustees sponsored a banquet and celebration with hundreds of people in attendance. After they had finished their first course, two policemen walked into the banquet hall and took George and Verda firmly by their arms, asking them to come outside. "We wondered," Verda said, "if there was a riot on the part of some students, unrest on the Redlands campus." Instead, they were shown a new Lincoln Continental, which their escorts told them was a farewell gift to them from the trustees.

Two effective presidential transitions which we came upon were those of Tom Fields at William Jewel College in Liberty, Missouri, and Weimer Hicks, previous president of Kalamazoo College in Michigan. Both men had had longer than average tenures and had held the banners of their institutions high. Fields expected to be rewarded handsomely in his departure from William Jewel, and the trustees had the money and obliged with a sizeable gift for retirement plus scholarships for grandchildren. The trustees of Kalamazoo were equally generous. Weimer had had a series of heart attacks which had disabled him for two years, but the Kalamazoo trustees hired an interim president and paid Weimer full salary during his recuperation. He was invited to return to the presidency, but his doctor advised against it. Instead, the Hickses were hired to the development staff at Kalamazoo, making contacts in any way they chose.

One of our most interesting visits was in Georgia with a nationally known educator. His presidency had won him many accolades and much respect as one of the finest college presidents and educators in America. Although he was not well, he arranged for the interview. When we reached the area, this ex-president was in the hospital. We found him distraught over happenings on the campus since his departure. "The new president is tearing down all the good things we tried to accomplish over the past decades. He wants to make his mark so badly that he feels even the proven good of the past must go, and he will replace it with his ideas. It's all a matter of ego." This man was going through real trauma on his deathbed over the breakdown of many sacred symbols and standards at a cause to which he had given his life. His situation left us heartsick.

One of the worst treatments we discovered was that of good friends who had headed a West Virginia college. During this presidency, the institution experienced giant steps in growth, facility expansion, and educational esteem. Both the president and his wife had talents for the unusual and the beautiful. Their commitment to Christian higher education was deep and real, but at the same time they were inclusive in their fellowship, as evidenced by their friendship with Ruth and me.

The joy of our friendship was saddened when the man, then president, had an automobile accident while traveling on college business. After months of hospitalization and recovery, he wanted to return to his post. Instead, he was asked to take early retirement. He obliged but asked for some financial settlement. The trustees felt that his retirement income should be enough and that the college had no further responsibility. He died a premature death and in a quiet ceremony was buried on his own property. His widow and children grieved in loneliness. Later, the college arranged for a memorial service to be held on the campus. I was asked to participate and did so gladly.

There is quite a difference in perspective and in degree of responsibility between a leader who has led an organization to a place of stability and even recognition, and one who has taken a successful enterprise and simply kept it going. Was that not the case with David and his son Solomon? David was not a perfect leader, but as the Bible states, "He was a man after God's own heart." He forged the nation of Israel by conquering their enemies both within and without. Solomon, who inherited the kingdom and the throne and became known for his wisdom as well as his riches, was talented and blessed, but he "lived too high on the hog," as the farmers say, and became irresponsible, and his reign ended in disgrace, and Israel was greatly weakened.

We would all like to think that in retirement we could have the great blessing spoken of by Isaiah (40:31).

Those who hope in the Lord shall renew their strength,
they shall mount up with wings as eagles,
they shall run and not be weary,
they shall walk and not faint.

TRUE RELIGION

I write this section somewhat fearfully, for it may be misinterpreted. However, it is an important part of my philosophy and of much of my ministry, both within the church and in the college presidency.

I always tried to tell students, "You'll never get to heaven on the faith of your fathers; only on what you make of faith and Christian life on your own. Don't be afraid of doubts. Look at your life and faith from all angles, but also remember not to stop halfway or to throw out the baby with the bath water." By the latter I meant that they should not throw out the old just because it's old. Real faith includes many eternal verities.

I must confess that several times in my ministry, and at one time particularly, I experienced a difficult time with so-called religious people. I actually feared talking with one lady who always spoke in religious language, even in normal conversation, because I thought she was more religious in verbiage than in action, and I feared the results. My worst contact, however, was with an older member of a church I pastored. He had a photographic memory and, more than anyone else I ever knew, could memorize the locations of Scripture. However, instead of using this talent beneficially, he used his knowledge to embarrass the teacher of the adult Bible class, who was an upstanding deacon and a fine instructor. The man in question, "Joe," embarrassed the teacher during a class session by asking where this or that Scripture could be found, and most times, the teacher was unable to answer specifically. When the class session closed, Joe would leave with his chin held high, believing that he was the superior Christian. After several years of pastoring that church, I found Joe also critical of me on the basis of the fact that I gave particular emphasis to the life and teachings of Jesus. I felt they were the key to what the Bible was all about, and I wanted to stress what Jesus himself taught and how he lived. It came to the point during one Holy Week when I felt Joe was going too far, doing actual damage in the church. I thought that if my Lord could wash the feet of Judas, knowing that he was going to betray him, I ought to be willing to wash Joe's feet. I took a pan and cloth and went to his home. I explained what I wanted to do, filled the basin half full of water, got down on my knees in front of him, and asked permission to remove his shoes. That wasn't easy, but I felt it was my pastoral duty to do so for the good of the church. Joe refused to cooperate, and of course I did not force the matter.

Much later, Joe was in a Charleston hospital, over a hundred miles from home, with a heart attack. I drove all the way there to have prayer with him and to let him know of my concern for his recovery. I'll never forget his words to me: "You mean you came all the way to see me?"

I answered, "Yes, Joe. You're a member of our church, and I'm your pastor. I want to have prayer with you and have you know of the love of our congregation." I felt my attempts at Christian outreach to him had an effect. He did not live long after that, and my tenure as pastor of the church also ended soon thereafter.

Again, I was trying to express my religion in personal, caring action, as opposed to religiosity based on words. I always felt Jesus had his hardest time with the religious zealots, the Pharisees and Saducees of his day, and that he felt more at home with some of the outcasts who were open to his message and love.

There were many fine, loving Christians in that church, and their care of their pastor and his wife was shown particularly after Ruth suffered her fatal fall in 1992. The kindness and concern of that congregation was a demonstration of what I believe to be the highest level of Christian faith.

MASTER TEACHER: DR. NORMAN VINCENT PEALE

THE IMPACT OF TEACHERS

Tribute must be paid to the impact of teachers, especially on my life. First of all, and before she was married to my father, my mother taught in a tiny school in Normalville in the mountains of western Pennsylvania. Teachers and ministers were always welcome in my home. My parents held them in high esteem. As a fairly serious student but not necessarily a brilliant one, I learned to do so, too. The transition from a two-room school in Poplar

Grove to a high school of 1200 students in Connellsville was a giant step for me socially as well as academically, for I still had the duties of a farm boy.

My early homeroom teacher, Emma Stewart, born in Indiana, Pennsylvania, and cousin of the famous movie star Jimmy Stewart, helped me to develop self-confidence, particularly in public-speaking. One day she came to me using my middle name (which my parents always used and by which I was known until I started dating Ruth, who said she liked my first name better and wanted to call me Dick). Miss Stewart said, "Eugene, we are going to have an extemporaneous-speaking contest. It will include all of the grades of the high school, and I would like to sponsor you as one of the contestants."

As I recall, I looked down at my toes with some embarrassment and said, "Miss Stewart, you don't know what you're proposing. I never participate well in that kind of situation."

She wasn't to be dissuaded but said further, "I'll work with you after school hours. We'll research the subject, and I'll guide you in practice. However, you must be willing to give the time and effort." I agreed to do whatever she thought would be successful, and I would share with my parents the fact that extra time would be needed.

We worked hard and, believe it or not, we won the contest. I say "we" because I felt she won it more than I did, but it took us both. That began my leadership role in several other lively aspects of high school life: the debate team, memorization of Scripture and sharing it in regular high school assemblies, the leading role in the class play "Smilin' Through."

My college life started in Philadelphia—six years in the combined program at Eastern Baptist College and Seminary located in Rittenhouse Square close to downtown Philadelphia. My favorite professors there were the dean, Carl Morgan, who taught my favorite subject, The New Testament, and Cubby Rutenber, who taught the social sciences. Unusual fieldwork assignments were given to each student, and since I excelled in music, several of mine were the leading of church choirs, including two years directing the choir at Green Hill Presbyterian Church in Wilmington, Delaware. Earlier, my roommate, Bob Acker, and I were assigned for two years to help missionary Grace Hatch in her work in downtown Camden, New Jersey. Every Thursday night we went across the Delaware River by subway and corralled as many youngsters as we could find wandering the streets. We brought them into a small gymnasium owned by the mission, taught them to play basketball, and always ended the evening with a worship service.

The Eastern experience was rich in many ways, and although the school was fairly new, life together was like family, and many of the friends I made there have continued most of my life.

In New Brunswick Seminary, to which I commuted from my first pastorate at the Central Baptist Church in Atlantic Highlands, I enjoyed the president, Dr. John Beardslee, who taught The Life and Teachings of Jesus and created from the Greek text his own version of the New Testament. It was there also that I became acquainted with the one I will call my favorite professor, Dr. Norman Vincent Peale. The story of that relationship will be found toward the end of this narrative.

At Columbia Teachers College, Ruth and I were both stimulated by the subjects we were taking in our doctoral programs. If we were to choose a favorite professor, it would be Dr. Phil Phenix, whose emphasis was on the importance of living "a life of loyalty, devotion, and love, and not the democracy of desire." In several classes of four hundred students, he still had the ability, as my wife said, "to shoot down the students who thought they were smart enough to challenge him."

I must add a tribute to Dr. Norman Vincent Peale, even though I took only several homiletics courses from him. He commuted to New Brunswick Seminary from New York by Pennsylvania Railroad, and I would often offer to take him back to the railroad station when classes ended. Because of this, we got to know each other personally.

I include him as one of my top "official" choices for several reasons. First, because he made such a strong impression on me and on many others through the force of his personality and his unique use of the English language. I offer a few illustrations.

1. One day, as I have heard the story, Dr. Peale was walking near his church when he met an old friend, "John." He said, "You really look down in the dumps today." John admitted that he had so many problems that he felt like giving up completely.

   Dr. Peale asked, "Would you like to get rid of a few of them or all of them?"

   John replied, "All of them."

   Dr. Peale said, "I can show you how you can get rid of them all, John. Come with me."

   Together they drove to the Bronx cemetery. As they got out of the car, Peale pointed all around and said, "John, here are several hundred thousand souls who have no problems. They're dead. You have problems because you're alive. Thank God for that!"

   John got the point and faced life with a new perspective.

2. One day a friend asked Dr. Peale what he would say to his son if he were on his death bed and wanted to share a final word. Dr. Peale answered very quickly, "I would tell him to get acquainted with Jesus, who truly is The Way, the Truth, and The Life." I think this response should satisfy some of the ministerial critics who felt Dr. Peale fell short of placing Jesus where he rightfully belongs.

3. A third incident I heard of involved two of Dr. Peale's friends who were enjoying lunch on Fifth Avenue. One asked the other, who was close to Dr. Peale, "How is Norman these days?" The answer will last in my memory as long as I live. "Norman is probably on his death bed, but he is fine. He has outlived many of his closest friends and out-loved all his enemies." I am thankful for Dr. Peale's challenge to my life and to those of many others of his ministerial students.

My final tribute is offered in memory of the teacher whom I knew best and lived with for forty-eight years. Ruth Mansberger Shearer was a teacher who excelled in being able to "put the fear of God in students when they needed it," at the same time letting them know she would do anything to help them succeed. She was a teacher who not only was the First Lady of Alderson-Broaddus College for thirty-three years but rightfully was named West Virginia Mother of the Year in 1974. She dedicated her energies with a deep spiritual commitment, as demonstrated by the following excerpts from her essay titled "Teaching as an Act of Reverence." It was published in the college magazine and elsewhere.

> Teaching to me is an act of reverence. It is not something I have to do to acquire the means for doing what I really want and like to do, for teaching is what I really *like* to do. It is not something I endure for nine months for the sake of one month in Europe. Rather, teaching provides a channel for devoted service. It is a means of maintaining things of value. It is a creative activity performed in obedience to the ideal of goodness. It is a way I can help others and show devotion to the Master Teacher.

> For one who has this attitude, teaching is not a burden, but a creative opportunity. It is a source of meaning. It

is an occasion of joy and enthusiastic participation in learning. The motive is not *getting* but *giving.*

Teaching out of devotion is justified not by *extrinsic* rewards but by the *intrinsic* value of the quality of the work itself. One who views teaching as an act of reverence is not likely to approach his work in a shoddy manner. Worship finds the worshipper at his best. He usually adorns both his body and his heart in special preparation for the act of reverence.

One of the courses I teach is educational psychology. At the last session of the term just before the bell rings marking the conclusion of the course, I read to the class my favorite quote about teaching written by William Lyon Phelps.

In my mind teaching is not merely a life work, a profession, an occupation, a struggle; it is a passion. I love to learn, I love to teach as a painter loves to paint, as a musician loves to play, as a singer loves to sing, as a strong man rejoices to run a race.

Teaching is an art—an art so great and so difficult to master that a man or woman can spend a long life at it without realizing much more than his limitations, his mistakes, and his distance from the ideal. But the main aim of my happy days has been to become a good teacher, just as every architect wishes to be a good architect, and every professional poet strives toward perfection.

As I read, the room becomes strangely quiet, the mood increasingly serious. For a moment at least the students seem to be caught up in the experience of what it can mean to be a truly devoted teacher.

I leave the room feeling hopeful because I sense that if these students can catch the vision of teaching as an act of reverence, nothing less than a revolution in the principles and practices of American education can take place, and this in turn can revolutionize the world. The challenge is overwhelming.

This is what my favorite, favorite, best known teacher believed and lived, and I agree with her with every fiber of my being. This was our—and my—life before, during, and to this very day. May it ever be so.

THE SHEARER FAMILY IN THE '80S
(L TO R BEHIND RUTH AND RICHARD:
PAT AND DICK WILSON, CANDY AND RICK
SHEARER, SUZIE AND TERRY JONES)

MEMORIAL DAY 2013

MEMORIAL DAY WAS ALWAYS SPECIAL for my family, both because it was the day of remembrance for our heritage and for all who had gone before us and also because, along with many other occasions in life, my dad was a very successful seller of monuments and grave markers, which he erected in many cemeteries, beginning in Connellsville. We always set aside the day to visit the cemeteries at the Indian Creek Baptist Church in Mill Run and also the Hillgrove Cemetery in Connellsville. Even in my older years, long after I moved away, I tried to honor this family tradition. Particularly after Ruth died in 1993, one or more of my children would try to take me to visit the Connellsville cemetery.

It had been several years since I had been able to go for this family memorial visit, but in 2013, at the age of 93, I was well enough to make the trip, and my daughter Suzanne encouraged me to do so and offered to take me. Her son Derek traveled from Nashville to Huntington and came up on Friday night, May 17, to help with the trip. I had made contacts. Specifically, I called two cousins, Linda Shearer, a teacher in a Connellsville high school, and my cousin John Shearer, who was retired and had lost his wife, Janet, about a month earlier.

In addition I contacted the couple living in the last house my father built in Poplar Grove, Jim Kirchoff and Deborah, in order to meet them for the first time.

We had lunch with John and Linda at Miedels' Restaurant in

the rural village of Poplar Grove. Those moments alone brought back many memories because I had grown up close to where we were visiting. While we were eating I told our guests and the waitress that when I was dating Ruth in our high school years, quite often in my visits to the Methodist parsonage where she lived in the center of town, I would try to think of something to give her as a token of my growing affection. Most times I would say, "Close your eyes and hold out your hand. I have a surprise for you," and then I would place a stick of Dentyne chewing gum in her hand. After we were married and really got to know each other, she often laughed and said she tried to show appreciation but had really longed for a Miedels' barbeque sandwich.

Her older sister, Betty, at the same time was dating her husband-to-be, Bill Shaw, who had a fairly good job with a rubber company, even in those Depression years. Ruth said when Billy came to see her sister Betty, he often brought just such a sandwich. My offering didn't compare, and in the restaurant sixty years later, my relatives and the waitress and I laughed together.

After lunch Suzie and Derek and I stopped nearby at the stone house my father had built amd that I now owned and rented to the Kirchoffrs. They were happy to see us and were proud of all the work they had done in repainting the house inside, getting ready to paint the outside. I had already given them several months' credit on their rent in order to provide this upkeep. They seemed very satisfied with our low rent and with their responsibility to take care of the home and keep it the most beautiful home of the area.

Of course, the main objective of the trip was to visit Hillgrove Cemetery. Linda Shearer maintains the lot beyond what the cemetery folks do themselves. Kenny, whom she knows well and who lives just across the street from the cemetery, helps. The location of the Shearer gravesite is very handy to Robbins Street. My father selected it and installed a lovely granite family monument. Most of my father's monuments came from a company in Vermont, where there is an extensive granite deposit. Linda had placed flowers in front and close to the monument. Flowers are prohibited at individual markers, a ruling of the cemetery association to make mowing easier.

First I stood by the main monument and looking at my mother's and father's markers, and my heart and mind lifted a prayer of thanksgiving. My mother died at 71 years of age of a heart attack, but my father lived ten years longer and married again. I'll never forget his coming with his long-time friend, Ethel Johnson, to Greystone, the president's home on the A-B College campus, and saying to Ruth and me, "Dear ones, I just can't live alone." And to me he said, "Will you marry us?"

As a minister of the Gospel before becoming the college president, I had a license to perform weddings, and I answered him not only affirmatively but enthusiastically. "I know you and Ethel have known each other, Dad. I think you can have some happy years ahead, and I will be happy to perform the wedding." We did just that within the next week.

I remember my father as one who had special gifts in dedication and determination. When he and my mother first came down from the mountain to Poplar Grove, they brought the farmer's way of life and rented a little forty-acre farm close to where I was born. In addition, however, during the Depression years my father engaged in a number of other business activities in order to keep the family well supplied and happy. Work, worship, and prayer were the three words that highlighted my growing-up years. Discipline was part of those years, but always love and care for family were given priority.

My memory as I stood before the gravesite included some sad moments, for there were markers around the family monument that indicated that I had a brother Karl, who died of diphtheria at the age of 6, before I was born. My sister, Ila Merlene, at the age of 9 helped to take care of me, then a baby. She died that year of meningitis. The medical community did not have the antibiotics to take care of such diseases. There were other family tragedies, like the nervous breakdown of my brother Paul when he was in his first job with the Firestone Company. My older brother, Howard, and his wife, Jenny, had two children stillborn, a harsh blow to their marriage. All of these memories came back as my eyes moved from marker to marker.

Above all, I want to emphasize again that my parents never grew bitter or blamed God. Instead they turned even more to prayer, worship in the church, and to helping others.

Brother Howard, ten years older than I, deserves special mention. One major event relates him to our early progress at A-B College. I knew we needed more students, above the 200 level of enrollment, if we were to survive. The business office was struggling already to meet bills and salaries, let alone put money into construction. Many of the schools around us had received Army surplus materials. I learned that Marshall University had benefited by the Army rebuilding several barracks units to house students. After using these for several years, Marshall was now wanting to replace them with permanent dormitories. The university advertised that they would give the old barracks to another college in the state.

I tried to find a contractor who would for reasonable cost do the job of tearing down the units at Marshall, transporting the materials to our campus, and reconstructing them. My search was in vain. However, when Howard heard of my dilemma, he said, "Dick, I think I could get three months off in the summer from my work in Pittsburgh to help you out." We both knew it wouldn't be an easy task, but Howard was determined to help the college and me. He went to Huntington and, luckily, made friends with Jim Hamer, CEO of the Hamer Lumber Company in Kenova. He and Jim called together a local team to tear down the five barracks units and have the salvageable material transported all the way to Philippi. Another team was developed in Philippi to rebuild three very usable units, increasing the college dormitory space by some ninety students. I always regretted that we did not have some sort of ceremony of appreciation for Howard.

As I stood at his grave this past month, I remembered his many kindnesses to my family and wished that he had had a happier family life. In his later years I was happy that Ruth and I went to Connellsville periodically, took him out to dinner and then to a playhouse performance in Scottsdale performed by the Fayette County Players. The last thing I remember his saying to me before he died was, "Dick, I wouldn't have had it any different." He was a great brother.

I went to Ruth's gravesite last. My daughter Suzanne, my grandson Derek, my cousin Linda and her helper-friend Kenneth were standing nearby. Many happy memories went through my mind. I was glad that Rudy and I had had forty-eight wonderful years together, glad that even amid original differences, we built a life of honor to the Lord, dedicated to Christian higher education at Alderson-Broaddus College.

While I stood at her grave I felt inspired to do again in my feeble way what I did sixty years earlier when we were married in the First Methodist Church of Weirton. She planned the wedding, and I took care of the honeymoon at Lake George, New York. She asked if, as a part of the wedding ceremony, while she stood at the back of the long aisle, I would sing as I stood in the front of the church with the ministers, her father, Dr. A.R. Mansberger, and my uncle, The Reverend Lindley Shearer, all in the presence of a church full of happy people. She had asked me to sing the wedding song, "Because." I did so with all the fervor I could muster.

While I stood at her grave, I remembered all this and commented to those around me, "I can't really sing well anymore, but I want to try to do that song again," and so I sang.

Because you come to me with naught save love And hold my hand and lift mine eyes above, A wider world of hope and joy I see Because you come to me.

Because God made you mine, I'll cherish thee And pray God's love will make our love divine Because God made you mine.

Suzanne said the song and the remembrance brought tears to her eyes, and I said, "I think mine were a little wet also, honey." I was happy we were together at the gravesite of my parental family and my dear wife, Ruth, for one last time.

Following the visit to the cemetery, Linda took us to the fairly new Connellsville High School to show us how the group she organized and now heads called the "Connellsville High School Patriots" had worked together for a number of years in honoring veterans. They had taken a trip to New York City and secured a piece of the World Trade Center that was destroyed on 9/11/01. It is attractively mounted in a large foyer at the entrance to the school of 1200 students, on a slab of concrete covered nicely with terrazzo. Linda has been selected for several years as Teacher of the Year. She is a graduate of Alderson-Broaddus College.

From there we went back to Miedels' restaurant for a quick lunch with Linda and with my other remaining cousin in Connellsville, John Shearer, whose daughter, Marjorie, also graduated from A-B. We visited the site where I was born in the little rural community and saw the forty-acre farm where my brothers and I picked apples, hoed corn, and shot at quails.

This memorable Mother's Day trip ended with Derek driving us back to West Virginia. It was a beautiful day, warm and memorable, like a good bowl of oyster stew welcoming me home. Memories of family last a lifetime and beyond, and I was content. I felt blessed, grateful for life, for family, and for faith. Suzie and I slept much of the way back to Philippi.

Made in the USA
Monee, IL
04 March 2022

92275739R00090